The New Illustrated
Bible Atlas

JOSEPH RHYMER

The New Illustrated
Bible Atlas

JOSEPH RHYMER

A QUINTET BOOK

Published by Chartwell Books Inc.,
A Division of Book Sales Inc.,
110 Enterprise Avenue,
Secaucus, New Jersey 07094

ISBN 0-89009-980-4

This book was designed and produced by
Quintet Publishing Limited
6 Blundell Street, London N7

Art Director Peter Bridgewater
Editor Suzanne Luchford

Typeset in Great Britain by
Central Southern Typesetters, Eastbourne
Colour origination in Hong Kong by
Hong Kong Graphic Arts Limited, Hong Kong
Printed in Hong Kong by Leefung-Asco
Printers Limited

The author and publishers are grateful to Ian Howes,
Sonia Halliday and Ronald Sheridan for supplying
the photographs.

Contents

Origins

Setting the Scene

The Bible makes vast claims for itself. It tells its readers that they can find the secrets of the universe within its pages, the whole pattern of history from the very beginning to the present day.

It opens with a picture of absolute, irresistible power. In six brief passages covering six days, it depicts the creation of the whole universe, and everything it contains, made to one single plan with mankind at its centre. It continues with explanations of the origins of evil, war, the struggle to earn a living, and the divisions between races and nations.

The opening chapters of the Book of Genesis are far more than descriptions of people, events and places. For Jewish and Christian believers they tell of God as he uses his cosmic powers to save mankind. Throughout the Bible God is playwright, director and actor in the drama of salvation, whose presence can be detected in everything that happens.

At the time when the Bible was first written, its readers were familiar with the events described, for they took place largely in their own times and their own country. In order to appreciate these writings today we need to discover all we can about the places where biblical events took place, and about the people who were involved in them.

Genesis

Genesis was written as an introduction to the main event in Hebrew history, the exodus, when the ancestors of the Hebrews made their escape from slavery in Egypt under the leadership of Moses. The escape itself and its immediate consequences are described in the books of Exodus, Leviticus, Numbers and Deuteronomy. The whole account was finally edited towards the end of the Old Testament period.

The final editors of these opening books of the Bible looked back over nearly 2,000 years of Hebrew history and saw how it had been shaped by its beginnings. The traditions which Jesus inherited as a Jew were deeply influenced by the exodus from Egypt, 13 centuries earlier, and by the stories of

ABOVE *Landscape with cranes. The creation is described as an ordered perfect whole in which everything – and everyone has its place.*

Abraham and his descendants four centuries before this. Genesis sets the scene for the whole Hebrew tradition and explains the forces at work in it.

An Ordered World

There are two accounts of the creation of the universe in Genesis. The first describes an ordered world with mankind as its administrator, where everything is part of one perfect plan. The second account is more primitive and personal as it explains the origins of sexual desire and sets the scene for the emergence of evil and enmity.

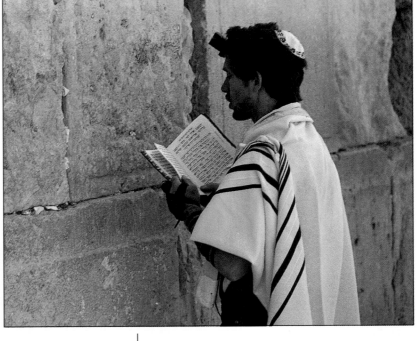

ABOVE *A Jew at the Western Wall, the most sacred place of prayer in the Jewish world. As a boy, Jesus himself inherited traditions which began 2,000 years earlier.*

Hebrew author of Genesis as he scraped a living in the harsh conditions of Palestine, for the Mesopotamian rivers Tigris and Euphrates are two of the four rivers which watered the Garden of Eden.

The great floods of Mesopotamia were models and reminders of the first, universal flood. When the waters subsided, Noah's ark grounded on the mountains of the Ararat range, north of Mesopotamia near the head-waters of the river Tigris.

Ancestors

The nomadic shepherd ancestor of all Hebrews, Abraham, entered Canaan (the earlier name for Palestine) about 1800 BC as he and his family moved their flocks along the traditional grazing routes between Mesopotamia and Egypt. The covenants God made with Abraham are enormously important, even today, for they are the basis of Hebrew claims to Palestine, 'The Holy Land', stretching from the Egyptian border to Syria, and from the Mediterranean coast to the eastern edge of the Jordan valley and the Dead Sea.

Subsequent chapters tell the story of Noah and the flood, the tower of Babel and the family tree of all mankind. They present God as just and merciful, as well as all-powerful, who preserves the continuity of creation after the flood and gives the first covenant to Noah. As Noah is the common ancestor of all mankind in these stories, this covenant is a promise of universal salvation to all people. In Hebrew and Christian tradition, the rest of the Bible shows how this promise was fulfilled.

The opening chapters of the Book of Genesis are set in Mesopotamia, the wide, fertile land of great rivers east of Palestine, beyond the deserts of Syria and Arabia. Mesopotamia seemed a paradise to the

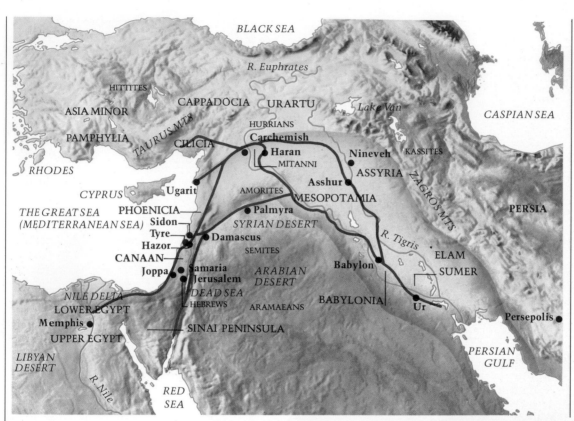

LEFT *The great arc of fertile land stretching from the Nile delta in Lower Egypt north through Palestine and then south and east to the Persian Gulf. The intrinsic fertility of the land in Palestine and its position on the narrowest strip of the fertile crescent meant that it was highly prized by both nomadic and settled agricultural peoples and made it a point of strategic importance to the local powers.*

'Fertile crescent'

Major trade routes

The stories about Abraham and his immediate descendants also connect the Hebrews with ancient Canaanite sanctuaries, which later became centres of the Hebrew religion. Even Jerusalem is mentioned, under its Canaanite name Salem, when its king brought gifts to Abraham. The city did not become the Hebrew capital until David captured it 800 years later.

The Canaanites were farmers who worked the fertile agricultural lands near their fortified settlements, while the Hebrew shepherds kept to the sparse grazing areas away from the 'cities'. Consequently, there was no direct competition between the nomadic Hebrews and the Canaanites at this time.

The Migration to Egypt

Egypt exercised a loose control over the region, particularly after 1640 BC when northern Egypt was captured by foreign rulers, the Hyksos, who were distantly related to the Hebrews. The Hyksos kings ruled

from Tanis and Avaris in the delta region of Egypt where the River Nile fans out into many channels as it enters the sea. Native Egyptians retained control of Upper Egypt south of the delta, which they ruled from Thebes.

This is the setting for the final chapters of Genesis, which describe the migation of the Hebrew shepherds to Egypt during a general famine. The main Hebrew figure is Joseph, who had been sold into slavery by his brothers and taken to Egypt, where he prospered and married the daughter of the high priest of the city of On (Heliopolis).

On, situated between Tanis and Avaris, was an important centre. The high priest of On bore the title 'Greatest of the Seers' and 'King's Son of his Body'. As a seer himself and the high priest's son-in-law, Joseph gained high rank in the Egyptian royal court where he could ensure that his Hebrew brethren would be welcome in Egypt.

The Hebrews settled in Goshen in the eastern part of the Nile delta, where they could escape the prolonged drought in their traditional grazing areas. But their fortunes would change when the native Egyptians dislodged (displaced) the Hyksos rulers a century later.

ABOVE Irrigation transforms arid desert into a garden; virtually the whole of Egypt's agricultural system depended on the waters of the River Nile.

LEFT The River Euphrates, one of the great rivers of the ancient world. Exploitation of the Euphrates in Mesopotamia for irrigation when the Hebrews arrived there was further advanced than it is today.

The Egyptians

There is virtually no rainfall in Egypt itself. The River Nile draws its waters from the highlands of Ethiopia and the tropical rain forests of central Africa. Consequently, Egypt could produce dependable crops, even when the whole of the eastern Mediterranean region was struck by drought. This was achieved by controlling the Nile's summer floods and by using irrigation channels to water the crops when the river level fell again in the autumn.

Egyptian rulers always found it difficult to maintain control over the whole country because of the contrast between the broad lands of the delta where the Nile entered the sea, and the narrow ribbon of fertile land, 600 miles (1000 km) long, either side of the river from the First Cataract to the delta. In the shifting patterns of Egyptian politics, power moved between Lower Egypt (the delta region) and Upper Egypt, between Memphis and Thebes, as different groups gained control and founded dynasties.

Divine Kings

The Egyptian king (the pharaoh) was himself a god and the earthly representative of the gods, but his authority was constantly undermined by the rich and powerful priesthood, even though the priests served the gods as representatives of the king. The country was administered by a highly organized bureaucracy manned by priests. The king's real power rested with the army which was an efficient, mobile force organized in units of 250 foot soldiers supported by light chariots.

Each administrative district had its own court of law, presided over by an official of the central government. As Egypt was ruled by a divine dictator there was no central code of law, but records were kept and decisions were influenced by precedents.

Egyptian religion regulated every aspect of the people's lives and subsequent death. Egyptian tombs were lavishly furnished with all that the dead would need during their journey through the underworld towards judgement: tools, furniture, weapons and food, and even houses, either real or as clay models. Some of the royal tombs, the pyramids, were already 15 centuries old when Abraham entered Egypt.

The country grew a wide range of crops: wheat for bread, barley for beer, cattle fodder, dates, citrus fruit, and vegetables for eating and for oil. Flax was cultivated for Egypt's famous linen, and the papyrus reed for paper.

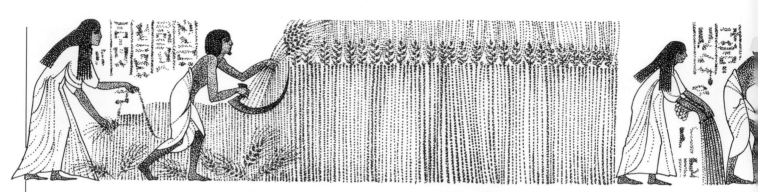

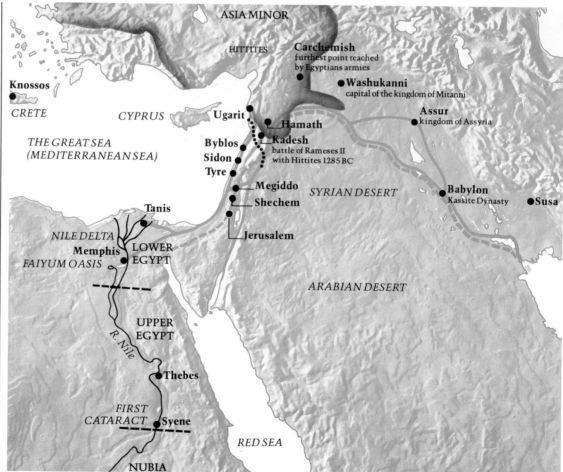

RIGHT *Egypt's prosperity depended as much on internal stability as it did on the wider regional balance of power. The strong Hittite kingdom to the north in Asia Minor and that of the Mittani in north west Mesopotamia limited Egyptian expansion even during times of relative domestic peace.*

— — — *Pasturage routes of Hebrew nomads*

• • • • • • • *Egyptian frontier under Rameses II in Syria*

▓▓▓ *Hittite empire*

——— *Major trade routes*

– – – *Frontiers*

ASIA MINOR

HITTITES

Carchemish furthest point reached by Egyptians armies

Washukanni capital of the kingdom of Mitanni

Knossos

CRETE

CYPRUS

Ugarit

Hamath

Assur kingdom of Assyria

THE GREAT SEA (MEDITERRANEAN SEA)

Byblos
Sidon
Tyre

Kadesh battle of Rameses II with Hittites 1285 BC

SYRIAN DESERT

Babylon Kassite Dynasty

Susa

Megiddo
Shechem

Tanis

NILE DELTA

Memphis
FAIYUM OASIS

LOWER EGYPT

Jerusalem

ARABIAN DESERT

UPPER EGYPT

R. Nile

Thebes

FIRST CATARACT **Syene**

RED SEA

NUBIA

Bundles of papyrus were lashed together and used to build boats for sailing the Nile, with their characteristic raised bows and sterns; they were often large enough for ocean voyages.

Slavery and Freedom

Fortunes changed dramatically for the Hebrew shepherds in Egypt when the foreign Hyksos kings were overthrown by native Egyptians. The Hebrews found themselves drafted into labour gangs to build frontier fortifications for the new dynasty. As the adopted child of an Egyptian princess, the Hebrew Moses might have been able to help but he had to flee Egypt after killing an overseer of Hebrew slaves.

Moses returned from his desert exile con-

ABOVE *A frieze showing a harvest in ancient Egypt, one of the world's major granaries at the time. Many of the tools and methods employed then are still in use in different parts of the world today.*

RIGHT *The Temple and Step Pyramid at Saqqara near modern Cairo. The temples of Egypt and the pyramid tombs of the pharaohs – divine kings – symbolized the absolute authority of the rulers and are now part of the most popular image of the country.*

vinced that God had chosen him to lead his people away from Egyptian rule to found a new nation. According to the Book of Exodus, Moses and his brother Aaron used the famous plagues to prove that the Hebrew God was more powerful than all the Egyptian gods, and forced the Egyptian Pharaoh to release the Hebrews.

The escape started with a celebration of the Passover, which was—and still is—the main Hebrew festival to which the other feasts are linked. Originally a protection rite for nomadic shepherds, Passover became the main commemoration of God's power to save his worshippers from any danger, and of his covenant with them.

The Covenant

Pursued by Egyptian soldiers, the Hebrews threw off the Egyptians in the salt marshes of the 'Sea of Reeds' (a better translation than 'Red Sea') and escaped into the desert areas east of the Nile delta. In order to avoid Egyptian troops on the coastal routes, and to reach the remote grazing lands of the nomadic shepherd tribes to which they were related, they turned south into the Sinai Peninsula.

Deep in the Sinai Peninsula, the Hebrews received the covenant with God at a sacred mountain. This confirmed their beliefs that the escape from Egypt was the supreme man-

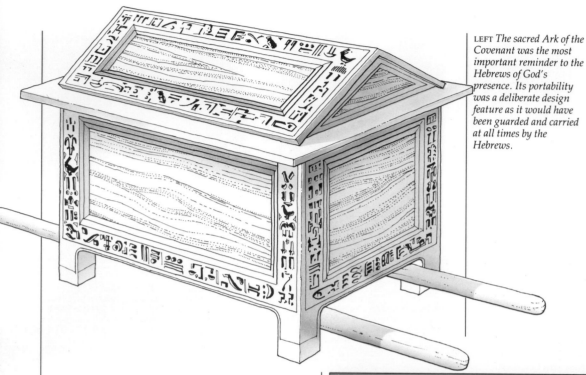

LEFT *The sacred Ark of the Covenant was the most important reminder to the Hebrews of God's presence. Its portability was a deliberate design feature as it would have been guarded and carried at all times by the Hebrews.*

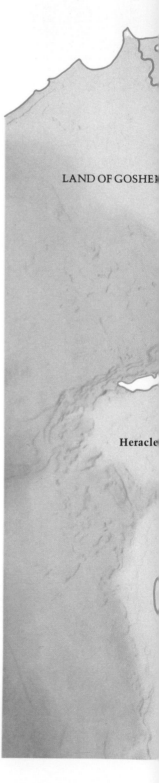

LAND OF GOSHEN

Heracle

ifestation of God's power and of his choice of them to be his special priestly people. For the Hebrews, these events gave ultimate authority to all their worship and law, by which they could express their gratitude and obedience to the God who had saved them.

Sacred Events

The Bible is essentially a record of sacred events rather than a book of abstract theological writings, and in each of its two major sections—the Old and New Testaments—there is an outstanding event to which everything else is related.

The escape from Egypt, the Exodus, is the outstanding event of the Old Testament, and the crucifixion and resurrection of Jesus form the corresponding event for the New Testament. The Bible makes it clear that neither of these events was fully understood at the time when they happened. The Exodus took place about 1250 BC, but it was at least seven centuries before the Hebrew people realized its full significance as a message of salvation to all the world. The crucifixion took place about AD 30, but some of the New Testament writers were still interpreting its significance nearly 70 years later.

ABOVE *Mount Sinai, deep in the southern Sinai Peninsula where the Hebrews received their covenant from God. The sacred mountain is now guarded by a fortified monastery.*

RIGHT *The escape, or exodus, of the Hebrews, led by Moses, from Egypt occurred in about 1250 BC through the marshes near the Mediterranean coast to the east of the Nile delta. The vicissitudes of the journey south through the Sinai Peninsula helped to forge the Hebrew identity.*

—— *Route of exodus*

—— *Major trade routes*

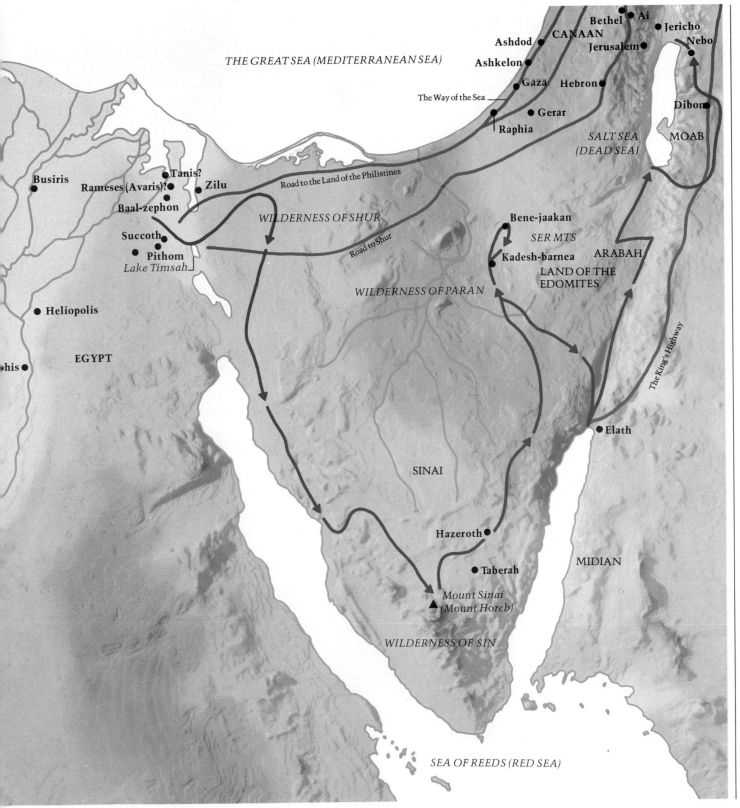

THE GREAT SEA (MEDITERRANEAN SEA)

Ai

Bethel

CANAAN

Ashdod

Jerusalem

Jericho

Nebo

Ashkelon

Gaza

Hebron

The Way of the Sea

Gerar

Dibon

Raphia

SALT SEA (DEAD SEA)

MOAB

Busiris

Tanis?

Rameses (Avaris)?

Zilu

Road to the Land of the Philistines

Baal-zephon

WILDERNESS OF SHUR

Bene-jaakan

SER MTS

Succoth

Road to Shur

Kadesh-barnea

ARABAH

Pithom

Lake Timsah

LAND OF THE EDOMITES

Heliopolis

WILDERNESS OF PARAN

his

EGYPT

The King's Highway

Elath

SINAI

Hazeroth

MIDIAN

Taberah

Mount Sinai (Mount Horeb)

WILDERNESS OF SIN

SEA OF REEDS (RED SEA)

A Communal Work

The contents of the Bible, as we know it, passed through many hands before it was written down. The stories were shared and preserved by word of mouth, together with explanations and comments which related them to ordinary, everyday life. They were part of the communal experience of history and of worship, which traced the effects of God's saving acts in the lives of the people who felt they had been influenced by them. There are no 'simple' descriptions of what happened, for they all reflect the beliefs of the people who recorded them, and are an integral part of those beliefs.

Consequently, it is difficult to say precisely when any part of the Bible was written, or when exactly the contents were edited into the book we now have. It is more important to appreciate the kind of lives the people lived, the countries they inhabited and the forces which shaped their societies. This is now easier to do, as archaeology uncovers more of the past and confirms the picture presented to us by the ancient biblical records.

ABOVE *Their escape from Egypt convinced the Hebrews of their own salvation and that God was more powerful even than the Egyptian gods represented by the great pyramids.*

RIGHT *The ancient port of Tyre linked the Near and Middle East with the Mediterranean world.*

Centres of Civilization

In ancient times, the two great centres of civilization in the middle east were located in Egypt and Mesopotamia. Between them lay parched desert and the Dead Sea, and the narrow land of Palestine which formed the only viable route for armies, trade and the nomadic shepherd peoples. Consequently, Palestine was always at the centre of international tension and strife.

South of Palestine lay Egypt traversed by the River Nile draining the tropics of eastern Africa. The rich agricultural lands made the area the most important source of food in the eastern Mediterranean. The people who drained the Nile marshes and maintained the irrigation canals created one of the oldest civilizations of the ancient world, whose engineering skills can still be admired 50 centuries later in the impressive ruins of pyramids and temples.

Beyond the Syrian and Arabian desert, east of Palestine, lay Mesopotamia, drained by the rivers Tigris and Euphrates. There too, civilizations arose from the skills learned in controlling the river floods and turning

ASIA MINOR
Byblos, Ugarit

Kadesh,
Hamath

MESOPOTAMIA
Damascus

*THE GREAT SEA
(MEDITERRANEAN SEA)*

Tyre

Kedesh
Hazor

Lake Huleh

BASHAN

Aduru

*SEA OF
CHINNERETH
(SEA OF
GALILEE)*

Acco
Achshaph

Karnaim
Ashtaroth

Mount Carmel ▲

Japhia

Yanoam

Wadi Yarmuk

Shunem

Megiddo

Beth-shan

Taanach

En-gannim

Pehel

Rehob

Dothan

Gath of
Sharon

Zaphon

R. Jabbok

Shechem ✚

Succoth

Penuel

Mahanaim

AMMON

Gath-rimmon

① Aphek

Joppa

CANAAN

Bethel
✚ Ai

Gezer

Aijalon

Jerusalem
(Salem)

Zorah

R. Jordan

SHEPHELAH

Ashdod

Gath?

Jarmuth

Bethlehem

Ashkelon

Libnah

Keilah

MOAB

Eglon

Lachish ✚ Hebron

Gaza

R. Arnon

Gerar Ziklag

Yurza

Beer-sheba
✚

②

EGYPT

*SALT SEA
(DEAD SEA)*

Kir-hareseth

PLAIN OF SHARON

them to agricultural needs. Despite its teeming population and great military powers, Mesopotamia was vulnerable to invasion from the mountain tribes to the east, so no single city or dynasty was supreme for long. As in Egypt, power in Mesopotamia moved up and down the river valleys.

Throughout this 'fertile crescent' from the Persian Gulf to Egypt, nomadic shepherds drove their flocks through the marginal lands between desert and the river valleys, owing allegiance to no one, amongst them were the Hebrews.

ABOVE *Palestine became the 'Holy Land' and the Hebrew sanctuaries there were some of the holiest places of all.*

✚ *Major sanctuaries associated with the Hebrews of Gen 12–50*

— *Major trade routes*

① *The Way of the Sea*

② *The King's Highway*

The Holy Land

Palestine gets its name from the Philistines who briefly controlled the narrow land-bridge at the end of the second millenium BC when they conquered it from the sea. The conquered natives were Canaanites living in independent, isolated hill fortresses. By 1000 BC the Hebrews had conquered both the Philistines and Canaanites to form the brief empire of Kings David and Solomon. For the Hebrews, this success was the final stage of the escape from Egypt and God's fulfilment of his covenant with them; from then onwards this would be the Holy Land.

The main international route from Egypt passed northward along the coast of Palestine to the ridge of Mount Carmel, where it split into an eastern branch to Syria and Mesopotamia. This branch skirted the Sea of Galilee while the western branch went to Tyre and Asia Minor. Palestine derived its prosperity and insecurity from this vital road and also exposed the Hebrews to an enormous range of cultural influences.

Apart from trade and war—for they were renowned mercenary soldiers—the Hebrews

RIGHT *The reliance of traders on pack animals to transport their merchandise tended to limit the major trade routes – which are particularly concentrated in and around Palestine – to areas of land which most readily supported life.*

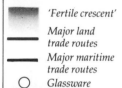

	'Fertile crescent'
—	Major land trade routes
—	Major maritime trade routes
○	Glassware
◈	Precious stones
⟋	Asphalt
♦	Corn
◊	Olive Oil
⬎	Metals
✕	Donkeys
♥	Figs
⫽	Silk
⦂	Wine
⬗	Textiles
⬣	Gold
◇	Copper
□	Tin
♣	Wood
■	Iron
✪	Frankincense
△	Dyes (especially purple)
▲	lead
▽	Ivory
𝍢	Papyrus
🐑	Wool
◆	Bronze
☆	Silver

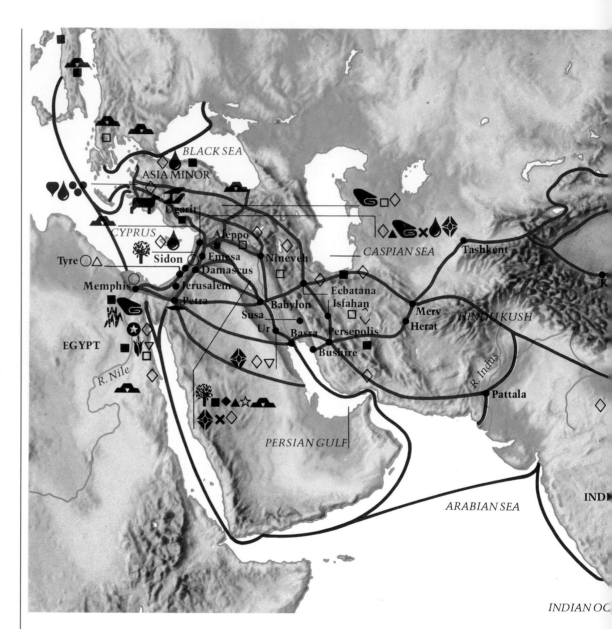

of ancient Palestine fell into two economic groups: the nomadic shepherds leading mobile lives, and the settled farmers of the fortified agricultural towns. As the Hebrews strengthened their hold over Palestine they turned more and more to farming. The change had profound consequences for their social and political patterns, and also for their religion.

The fortified settlements of the farming communities had a social structure based on land ownership, with pyramids of power capped by the kings of the various 'cities'.

The bulk of the peple existed as landless slaves owned by the farming and military classes, and all of them ruled by kings with absolute powers. As the Hebrews became farmers, so they turned to this way of life.

The New Way of Life

The Canaanite farmers of Palestine worshipped a host of gods and goddesses all related to the needs of a farming community. The

ABOVE *The cultivation and drainage of the marshes of the Rivers Tigris and Euphrates were important early stages in the civilizations of Mesopotamia.*

BAY OF BENGAL

probable Chinese route

main theme was the fertility of the land, which was secured by the sexual intercourse between the gods and goddesses. This was re-enacted between priests, priestesses and people in religious rites to ensure the fertility of the crops. Human sacrifice was also practised to secure the fertility of the fields or to avert military disaster. The main festivals were associated with the cycle of the agricultural year, from sowing to harvest. Each city had its temple, and there were sanctuaries in groves of trees and on hills.

As the Hebrews became farmers, they turned to this type of religion which seemed so necessary to life in Canaan. Much of the Old Testament is concerned with the struggle to adapt the Hebrew religion of the Exodus and covenant to the new way of life. As nomadic shepherds, the Hebrews had lived as close-knit families which formed the basis for clans and tribes. There was little difference of class where the flocks belonged to the whole family, and the heads of families were the natural patriarch-rulers.

The old Hebrew religion of the Exodus emphasized God as Father, and the essential quality and value of everyone in the community, for all of them were 'people of the covenant'. They worshipped at a portable shrine, the 'ark of the covenant', which they carried with them and there was no separate priestly class. Eventually the two systems of belief were reconciled and the old Hebrew religious values prevailed, but only after centuries of struggle during which prophets withstood (endured) the corruption of Hebrew kings and priests, often at the cost of their lives.

The Fertile Country

The great hill fortress of Megiddo is typical of many Canaanite cities, and of Hebrew cities after the Canaanites had been conquered. Like Jerusalem, Megiddo's thick walls and cunningly (cleverly) designed gate defended a rocky hill with storage pits for grain and a shaft and tunnel which gave access to the city's water supply during times when the city was besieged.

As in Egypt and Mesopotamia, the main crops of Palestine were wheat and barley, commemorated in the feasts of Unleavened Bread and Weeks (Pentecost). Dates, olives, grapes, citrus and a range of other fruits and vegetables were cultivated wherever water was found or land irrigated. Almost everywhere in Palestine is fertile if water can be provided, and excavations have shown that far more of the country was cultivated, through elaborate irrigation schemes, than was once thought possible.

Even near the Dead Sea, freshwater springs made for tropical luxury in such ancient centres as Jericho. The springs made it possible to maintain comfortable settle-

ABOVE The Canaanite farmers of Palestine believed that the fertility of their fields depended on the faithful worship of the Caananite fertility gods and goddesses.

FAR RIGHT The code of Hammurabi, King of Babylonia during the 17th century BC, was one of the most influential codes of laws in the ancient Middle East.

RIGHT Southern Palestine is relatively arid compared to the north where the mountains catch the rain carried by the westerly winds. The rainfall in the mountains runs off into the Jordan valley.

ments on the western shores of the Dead Sea in biblical times. Where springs were lacking or inadequate, the inhabitants dammed the deep gullies of the rift valley through which the River Jordan flows to the Dead Sea. The water was then channelled to their towns. We can begin to see why the Bible describes Palestine as 'a land of wheat and barley, of vines, of figs, of pomegranates, a land of olives, of oil, of honey. . . a land where stones are of iron, where the hills may be quarried for copper. . . where your flocks and herds increase'.

The Struggle for Palestine

But the people of Palestine, whether Canaanites or Hebrews, were seldom left in peace. As the patterns of domination waxed and waned in Mesopotomia and Egypt, Palestine usually found itself a centre of contention as one power or another saw it as a frontier area essential to its security. It was free from occupation by foreign powers less than 200 years out of 2,000.

In Mesopotamia, the Sumerian civilization

THE GREAT SEA
(MEDITERRANEAN SEA)

ASIA MINOR

MESOPOTAMIA

Damascus

Jezzine

Mount
Hermon

Tyre

Dan

Lake Huleh

Hazor

Acco

SEA OF CHINNERETH
(SEA OF GALILEE)

Mount Carmel

Nazareth

Ashtaroth

Wadi Yarmuk

Megiddo
Aruna

Beth-shan

Ramoth-gilead

Jezreel

Jenin

PLAIN OF
SHARON

Samaria

HILL COUNTRY
OF EPHRAIM

Shechem

Mahanaim

Joppa

Aphek

Shiloh

Bethel

Rabbah

Jericho

Heshbon

Ekron

Ashdod
Gath?

Jerusalem
(Jebus)

Ashkelon

Bethlehem

Zereth-shahar

HILL COUNTRY
OF JUDAH

Gaza

Eglon

Lachish

Hebron

Dibon

En-gedi

PLAIN OF
PHILISTIA

SHEPHELAH

SALT SEA
(DEAD SEA)

Beer-sheba

EGYPT

THE NEGEB

Kir-hareseth

R. Jordan

---	Regional rainfall:	④	Above 50in (1300mm)	④	The Eastern Hills
①	0–15in (0–400mm)	---	Natural regions:	⑤	The Desert
②	15–30in (400–800mm)	①	The Coastal Plain	ⓐ	The Way of the Sea
③	30–50in (800–1300mm)	②	The Western Hills	ⓑ	The King's Highway
		③	The Rift Valley		

was already in decline when Abraham left her borders in about 1800 BC. Babylon was rising as the dominant power under the leadership of King Hammurabi, and soon conquered every district of Mesopotamia and Syria from the Gulf to the Mediterranean. The Babylonians failed to penetrate into Palestine as Egypt strengthened its hold over the Canaanite cities. Before they were overthrown by the Kassites, they left a legacy of a great legal code and epic religious myths. The Babylonian creation legends and the 'Epic of Gilgamesh' undoubtedly influenced the opening chapters of the Book of Genesis, even though the Hebrew authors transformed the materials as they used them.

Contending Powers

For a brief period, around the time of the Hebrew migration to Egypt, the Hittites of

Asia Minor seemed set to dominate the area north of Palestine. Egyptian control was sustained, particularly by the Hyksos rulers, and the contending powers of Mesopotamia, including the Assyrians, were too weak to challenge Egypt. The time came when the Assyrians conquered the whole of the middle east, but this was not until five centuries after the Hebrew escape from Egypt.

Egypt might have taken advantage of the struggle for power in Mesopotamia during the period between Abraham and the Hebrew Exodus, the middle part of the second millenium BC, but she was torn by internal strife. For nearly a century, northern Egypt and Palestine were ruled by the invading Hyksos, but even when the native Egyptians regained control there was no internal stability for long.

The Religion of Egypt

As religion played such a central part in Egyptian life, so too it was a focus for power struggles. Although the Egyptian king was worshipped as the divine mediator between the gods and the people of Egypt, the priests of the many gods exercised enormous power as the country's administrators and intellectuals.

The main theme in Egyptian religion, expressed particularly in the architecture and orientation of pyramids, stelae and temples, was the worship of the sun. The rising of the sun was the source of creation and renewal, while the journey of the sun god through the underworld during the night reflected the pattern of death and regeneration. It was a religion full of meaning for an agricultural people.

About a century before the Hebrew exodus from Egypt, King Akhnaton tried to impose a single, uniform religion and government on the people of Egypt by suppressing all expressions of religion except the worship of the sun. The priests defeated his attempts at religious reform and the monuments to his monotheism were defaced after his death, possibly during the rein of the young Tut'ankhamun. Egypt never succeeded in extending her power far beyond her borders because of the problem of maintaining internal unity.

ABOVE *The sphinx was a mythical beast, a composite of a lion's body and a human head. The head of the Great Sphinx is that of King Knafra of the 4th dynasty.*

Origins

BELOW *The Great Sphinx at Al Jizah, sculpted from natural rock, is perhaps the single most monumental expression of the divine authority of the rulers of ancient Egypt, although its original meaning is not altogether clear.*

CHAPTER 2

Conquest of Palestine

Philistines

As the Hebrews, newly escaped from Egypt, wound their way through the desert areas south of the Dead Sea towards Palestine, near the end of the thirteenth century BC, the region was unusually free from control by any of the great international powers.

Normally, Egypt kept a close watch over Canaan (soon to become known as 'The Land of the Philistines' — Palestine) through client states and military patrols, but the Philistines were attacking Egypt from the sea and the Egyptians were fully occupied in repulsing them. The Philistines successfully invaded Canaan, and established five cities as their base—Gaza, Ashkelon, Ashdod, Gath and Ekron—before imposing their rule over the rest of the country. Egypt was powerless to interfere as she was weakened by internal conflicts between the Pharaoh and the powerful, wealthy groups of priests who controlled local districts of Egypt.

The great states to the north of Palestine, in Asia Minor, and to the east in Mesopotamia failed to take advantage of Egyptian weakness and control Palestine; they too were incapa-

BELOW *The ancient Egyptians defeated the Sea Peoples or Philistines at a great naval battle, but they could not stop them from establishing themselves in Palestine.*

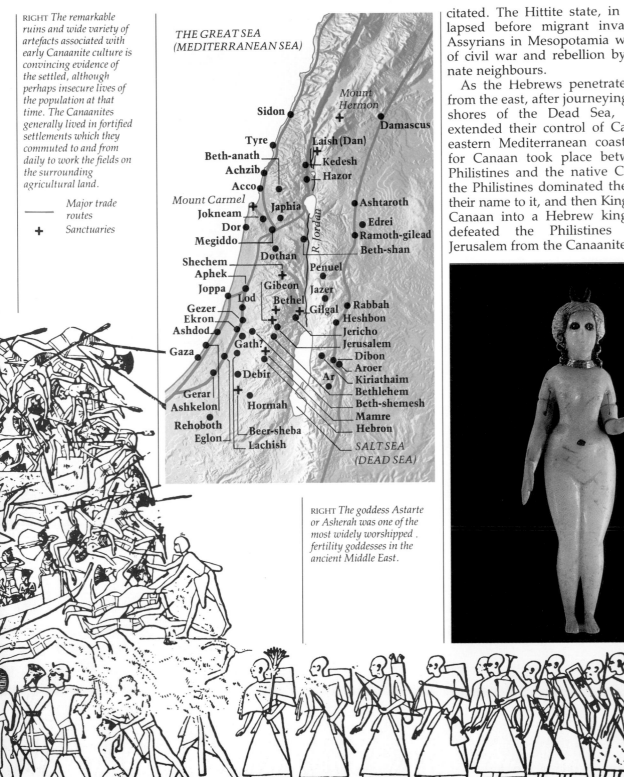

RIGHT *The remarkable ruins and wide variety of artefacts associated with early Canaanite culture is convincing evidence of the settled, although perhaps insecure lives of the population at that time. The Canaanites generally lived in fortified settlements which they commuted to and from daily to work the fields on the surrounding agricultural land.*

— Major trade routes

✛ Sanctuaries

THE GREAT SEA (MEDITERRANEAN SEA)

Mount Hermon

Sidon
Damascus
Tyre
Laish (Dan)
Beth-anath
Kedesh
Achzib
Hazor
Acco
Mount Carmel
Ashtaroth
Jokneam
Japhia
Edrei
Dor
Ramoth-gilead
Megiddo
Beth-shan
Dothan
Shechem
Penuel
Aphek
Joppa
Gibeon
Jazer
Lod
Bethel
Rabbah
Gezer
Gilgal
Heshbon
Ekron
Jericho
Ashdod
Gath?
Jerusalem
Gaza
Dibon
Aroer
Debir
Ar
Kiriathaim
Gerar
Bethlehem
Ashkelon
Hormah
Beth-shemesh
Mamre
Rehoboth
Beer-sheba
Hebron
Eglon
Lachish
R. Jordan
SALT SEA (DEAD SEA)

RIGHT *The goddess Astarte or Asherah was one of the most widely worshipped fertility goddesses in the ancient Middle East.*

citated. The Hittite state, in the north, collapsed before migrant invaders, and the Assyrians in Mesopotamia were in the grip of civil war and rebellion by their subordinate neighbours.

As the Hebrews penetrated into Canaan from the east, after journeying up the eastern shores of the Dead Sea, the Philistines extended their control of Canaan from the eastern Mediterranean coast. The struggle for Canaan took place between Hebrews, Philistines and the native Canaanites. First the Philistines dominated the area and gave their name to it, and then King David, turning Canaan into a Hebrew kingdom when he defeated the Philistines and captured Jerusalem from the Canaanites in 1000 BC.

Canaanites

The Canaanites whom the Hebrews conquered were a mixture of peoples, from the seafaring Phoenicians of the northern coast to the farmers of the south, but there was a strong cultural unity among them. Compared with the Hebrews they were advanced in technology and literature. Canaanite scribes developed the first true alphabet, which passed from pictorial writing to the more flexible single-letter scripts which were eventually adopted throughout the middle east and, in due course, the world. Its secret was the use of vocal sounds, the smallest components of words, as the basic units for the alphabetical scripts.

The Canaanite way of life, including their religion, revolved round the basic needs of farming and defence. They worshipped a complex pantheon of gods and goddesses, of whom the most important were El, the father of the Gods, and the goddess Asherah. Baal, son of El and Asherah, is frequently denounced in the Old Testament as a threat to the purity of Hebrew religion, a sure indication that many Hebrews were attracted by Canaanite worship.

City-States

Like the Greeks in their city-states, the Canaanite cities were frequently at war with each other, and Canaanite history reveals a shifting pattern of alliances and enmities between the various small states. The Canaanite cities were hill-top strongholds, heavily fortified against other Canaanite cities, scattered across the parts of Palestine capable of being farmed. With no central organization or government, the Canaanites fell first to the Philistines and then to the Hebrews.

The Hebrews were deeply influenced by the Canaanite way of life. They adopted some of the language and symbolism of Canaanite religion, particularly the name El for God, and aspects of the Canaanite creation stories. As Hebrew worship developed, it adopted rites and festivals associated with the Canaanite agricultural year: the main

	OX	HOUSE
EGYPTIAN HIEROGLYPHICS *c3000* BC		
CANAANITE *c2000* BC		
PHOENICIAN *c1000* BC		
HEBREW *c700* BC		
OLD GREEK *c650* BC		
ARAMAIC *c350* BC		
FORMAL HEBREW *c150* BC		
FORMAL GREEK *c450* BC		
ROMAN *c550* BC		

harvest festivals (which the Hebrews then related to the power God had demonstrated when he rescued them from the Egyptians), and the sacrifice of animals, crops and incense as burnt offerings and communion meals.

The Old Testament roundly condemns the Canaanite fertility rites as sacred prostitution, and the terrible sacrifice of children to the god Molech. It is clear that these practices were widespread among Hebrews as they adopted the Canaanite way of life. During the height of the Hebrew monarchy a shrine to Molech was built outside Jerusalem, and at least two of the Hebrew kings sacrificed their sons there in times of national danger.

ABOVE *The Canaanite scribes invented the first alphabet, from which all Western systems of writing were derived.*

WATER	EYE	HEAD	PAPYRUS	
ν η	◉	🗿	⊎	Egyptian writing did not develop far from the use of pictorial symbols.
	☓	ꓔ	ⱳ	Canaanite writing shows its pictorial origins, but in fact symbolizes basic sounds.
₹	○	ꓤ	Ш	The 22 basic symbols of the Canaanite system became the standard for the region.
₹	○	ꟼ	ⱳ	The Hebrews adopted the Canaanite alphabet in a modified form.
ᄀ	▯	ꟼ	Ƨ	The Canaanite origins can still be seen in archaic Greek script.
ᄁ	∪	ꓶ	ⱱ	Aramaic was the main language of the Persian Empire, and displaced Hebrew in Palestine.
ᄁ	ᄼ	ꓶ	Ɱ	Classical Hebrew was written in a 'square' form of the common script of the region.
ᄁ	O	P	Σ	The Greek alphabet allocated vowel sounds to some of the letters, and added more symbols.
ᄁ	O	R	S	The Romans gained their alphabet from the Etruscans and Greek colonists.

RIGHT *The strength of the fortifications which constitute the ancient fort of Jericho (Hebrew for 'fragrant') were dramatically revealed when archaeologists unearthed one of the great corner forts of its walls.*

Temples

The architecture of Canaanite temples strongly influenced Hebrew religious buildings. The excavations at the temple in Hazor in northern Palestine reveal a succession of rectangular rooms leading to a large, innermost sanctuary with a carved square altar displaying the symbol of the storm god, Baal, and a seated statue. Two pillars situated between the temple porch and the middle chamber served no structural purpose and must have been used in the Canaanite religious rites. This pattern is very similar to the Temple King Solomon built in Jerusalem as

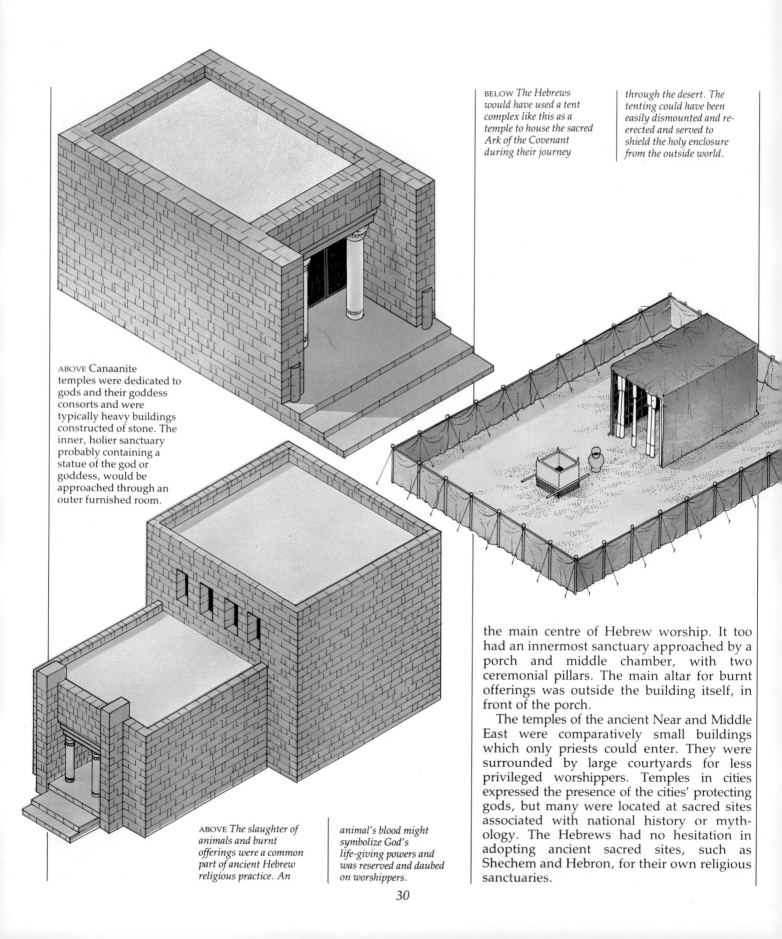

ABOVE Canaanite
temples were dedicated to
gods and their goddess
consorts and were
typically heavy buildings
constructed of stone. The
inner, holier sanctuary
probably containing a
statue of the god or
goddess, would be
approached through an
outer furnished room.

BELOW The Hebrews
would have used a tent
complex like this as a
temple to house the sacred
Ark of the Covenant
during their journey
through the desert. The
tenting could have been
easily dismounted and re-
erected and served to
shield the holy enclosure
from the outside world.

ABOVE The slaughter of
animals and burnt
offerings were a common
part of ancient Hebrew
religious practice. An
animal's blood might
symbolize God's
life-giving powers and
was reserved and daubed
on worshippers.

the main centre of Hebrew worship. It too
had an innermost sanctuary approached by a
porch and middle chamber, with two
ceremonial pillars. The main altar for burnt
offerings was outside the building itself, in
front of the porch.

The temples of the ancient Near and Middle
East were comparatively small buildings
which only priests could enter. They were
surrounded by large courtyards for less
privileged worshippers. Temples in cities
expressed the presence of the cities' protecting
gods, but many were located at sacred sites
associated with national history or myth-
ology. The Hebrews had no hesitation in
adopting ancient sacred sites, such as
Shechem and Hebron, for their own religious
sanctuaries.

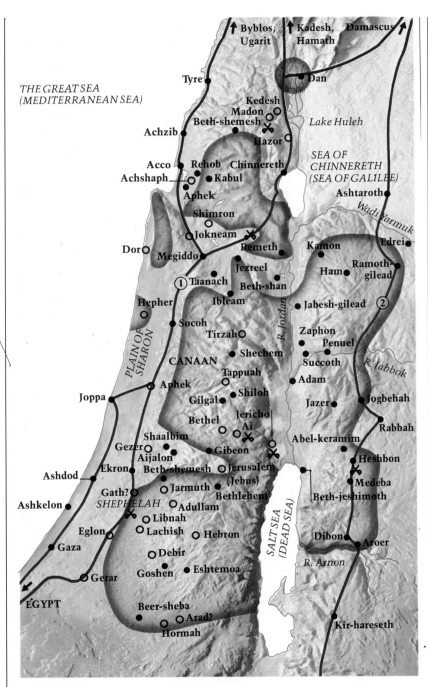

Divine Rights

The Book of Joshua presents a dramatic account of the Hebrew conquest of Palestine. A more difficult consolidation period followed, which is recorded in the Book of Judges, when the Philistines controlled the land. These accounts emphasize that God had given the land to the Hebrews, and that national security depended on strict obedience and loyalty to God. The divine rights of the Hebrew people as God's chosen are a prominent theme, both here and in other Old Testament writings.

An analysis of the lists of Canaanite cities and kings given in the Book of Joshua (places conquered by the Hebrews, places where they failed, and lists of the territories eventually allocated to the various Hebrew tribes) show that the occupation proceeded in three phases.

First the Hebrews took Jericho in the Jordan Valley, and then they moved into the Judean hill country south of Jerusalem. At this stage Jerusalem was too strong to capture and it did not become a Hebrew city until two centuries later when King David made it his capital. In the next phase they took the hill country north of Jerusalem, and the coastal plain of Sharon north of Joppa. Finally, there were the wars of the northern cities, including the great trading centre of Hazor on the road to Damascus and Mesopotamia.

Subjugation

The campaign was more of an infiltration than a conquest, in which the Hebrews neutralized Canaanite opposition as they occupied the marginal lands between the city territories, by defeating coalitions of Canaanite kings. In all, the full occupation took a century and a half to complete, and was not secure until the Hebrews defeated the Philistines in the time of King David. Until they adopted Canaanite farming methods, the nomadic Hebrew shepherds could co-exist with the Canaanite farming settlements, as they were not competing for the agricultural land. By the time of David, the Hebrew way of life had changed so much

ABOVE The Hebrews infiltrated Canaan only gradually, at first occupying the most sparsely populated land neglected by the Canaanites. Once the Hebrews were settled, numerous and united enough, they began to overrun the cities, a trend the poorly organized Canaanites could do very little about.

○ Conquered cities

— Major trade routes

① The Way of the Sea

✕ Sites of conflicts

Regions of early Hebrew settlements

② The King's Highway

that they had to subjugate the Canaanites and Philistines, or be subjugated by them. This is the true significance of King David's success, and the source of his outstanding reputation as the founder of the main Hebrew dynasty.

The Book of Judges tells of the deeds of 12 'judges', who rallied various combinations of the Hebrew tribes and organized them to resist attacks by the Canaanites or enemies beyond the borders of Palestine. Their success in a military crisis gave them extraordinary authority as people filled with God's power and wisdom, and they continued to exercise this authority after peace had been restored. For most of this period the Hebrews continued to live as independent tribes with no central organization to unite them, except for the central sanctuaries where the sacred Hebrew Ark of the Covenant was housed at

ABOVE *The heavily fortified Canaanite hill-top cities were the last pockets of resistance in Palestine to fall to the Hebrews.*

various times, particularly Shechem and Shiloh. The Hebrew tribes who settled in the northern parts of Palestine seem to have had little contact with those settled in Judah, who adopted Hebron as their main sanctuary, and between the two there was a belt of Canaanite cities, including Jerusalem, where the Hebrews had not established a foothold.

Enemies

Apart from the Canaanites, who were too weakened by inter-city wars to dislodge the Hebrews, other enemies of the Hebrews are named as the Edomites, Moabites and Ammonites. They were located on the international route which passed northwards along

the eastern side of the Dead Sea and the Jordan valley. This was the route taken by the Hebrews on their way to Palestine from Egypt, and was the traditional route for the nomadic shepherds. The Midianites are named as another enemy, and since this was the nomadic tribe which had helped the Hebrews during their escape from Egypt, mention of them shows that the Hebrews had become settled people who had begun to resent the incursions of nomadic shepherds!

With the final chapters of the Book of Joshua, and the First Book of Samuel, the history reaches the struggles of the Hebrews against the Philistines as they tightened their control of Palestine from the Philistine coastal cities of Gaza, Ashkelon, Ashdod, Gath and Ekron. In these stories, Samson is the most colourful of the judges, even though he was eventually unsuccessful against the Phili-

ABOVE *David had to flee for safety to the desert region of Judah to escape Saul's jealousy.*

stines. Behind the vivid folk legends, we can glimpse a resistance fighter who organized a small guerrilla war against the Philistines in the hill country of Judah, and was not afraid to penetrate occasionally into the Philistine strongholds themselves.

At the central sanctuary of Shiloh, north of Jerusalem, the Ark of the Covenant was tended by a Hebrew priestly family, headed by Eli. Here the young Samuel was dedicated to the service of the shrine by his parents. Samuel would have been serving there when the Hebrews carried the sacred Ark into battle against the Philistines at Aphek, around the year 1050 BC. The Hebrews were defeated, the Philistines captured the Ark and Shiloh was destroyed. Samuel went on to be the last of the charismatic leaders of the Hebrews before the real emergence of the Hebrew monarchy.

Saul, the First King

Defeat by the Philistines showed the Hebrews that the old, informal federation of Hebrew tribes could no longer defend the people now that they had settled in permanent locations. They needed a recognized, central ruler, and Samuel organized the anointing of Saul as the first Hebrew king.

Perhaps the new form of government was too great a change, particularly while Samuel was still a powerful force, and Saul did not command the loyalty of the southern Hebrew tribes. Saul clashed with Samuel, and then was defeated by the Philistines near Mount Gilboa in the valley of Jezreel and committed suicide. David had served in Saul's court and had already acquired a powerful military reputation and a band of followers. Saul's death gave David his opportunity to become the king who first united the Hebrew people and gave them security by defeating the Philistines.

David

Bethlehem, the most northerly town in Judah and just south of Jerusalem, first became famous as the birthplace of David. It was from Bethlehem that the young David went to King Saul's court as a page and army officer. With King Saul's defeat by the Philistines and subsequent death, David was able to secure the support of both the northern and the southern groups of Hebrew tribes, and was anointed king in Saul's place by both groups.

David emerged as an astute politician of many talents. The lament he wrote for Saul and his son Jonathan after the Battle of Gilboa reveals David as the poet who wrote at least some of the psalms. David's political stature is shown by the skill with which he commanded the loyalty of the many different groups among the Hebrews. He finally reinforced his position as king of all the Hebrews by choosing as his capital a city which had no previous political or religious associations for any of the Hebrew tribes, Jerusalem.

RIGHT *David was the first king of a united Palestine and made Jerusalem, a neutral city, his capital. He was first accepted by the southern Hebrews and then by the northern tribes and with the nation behind him assumed firm control over the land of Israel and the trade routes passing through it. Carefully chosen governors ruled the subservient states outside the areas of David's direct rule.*

● *Philistine cities*

+ *Sanctuaries during the early monarchy*

◉ *Cities strengthened by King Solomon*

The Land of Israel

Conquered region under Israel's rule

Region under vassal treaty

— *Major trade routes*

LEFT *The Gihon spring was ancient Jerusalem's only water supply and essential to the city's successful defence. David's troops eventually captured the city by entering via the spring's access shaft.*

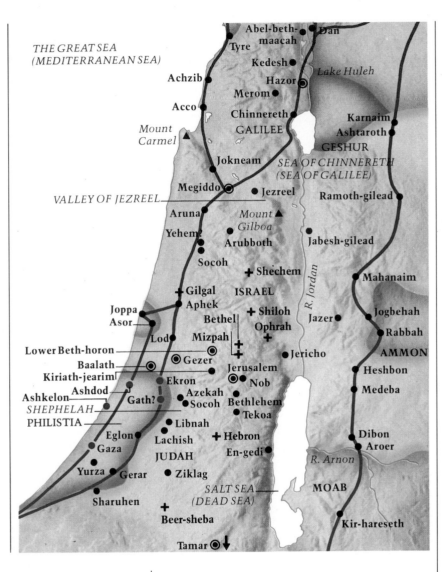

David captured Jerusalem from its Canaanite citizens and made it the national religious centre for Hebrews by installing the sacred Ark of the Covenant in it.

By defeating the Philistines, King David not only gave his people national security in Palestine, he also gained control of the great international trade routes which had to pass through the area. He established his rule from Damascus to the Egyptian border, and from the Great Sea (the Mediterranean) to the Syrian desert. The Hebrews had won a small empire centred on Palestine. David's descendants inherited his throne by divine right as guardians of the covenant with God, and for the first time the Hebrews could look forward to a secure future.

Solomon's Temple

That future was not without its problems, particularly about religion. From the time of David's son and successor, King Solomon, tensions began to emerge between Hebrews who remained loyal to the old religion of the desert and the nomadic shepherds, and Hebrews who accepted the new political, economic and social structures. Much of this tension was focused on the new Temple built by Solomon in Jerusalem to house the Ark of the Covenant. The Temple symbolized the change from the old nomadic religion when the Ark travelled with the tribes in its own tent, to this new religion of settlements.

The new Temple in Jerusalem showed that at least some Hebrews had adopted the Canaanite way of life, with its fortified cities, its agricultural economy and its monarchical form of government. The Temple was not only the shrine of the Ark, it was also the royal chapel administered by priests who were appointed by the king.

The plan of the Temple confirmed this, for it was very similar to other temples in Canaanite areas. A small building, it was at most 150 feet (50 m) long by 60 feet (20 m) wide, and stood in the great court of the royal place with its own inner court. The two connecting chambers of porch and main hall led on into the innermost shrine which housed the Ark of the Covenant.

ABOVE *The imposing site of the great Temple built by Solomon on The Dome of the Rock in Jerusalem is now occupied by an impressively beautiful Islamic shrine.*

The Great Altar

The main hall contained an altar for burning incense, a table for the 'bread of the presence', and 10 lampstands. The main focus for worship stood in front of the Temple building, the great bronze altar of whole burnt offerings, a raised hearth 30 feet (10 m) square and 15 feet (5 m) high, on which the main sacrifices were made. The sacrificial animals, slaughtered nearby where channels drained away the blood, were carried by priests up a flight of steps to the fire which burnt perpetually on the altar. Near the altar was a bronze water basin 15 feet (5 m) in diameter and 8 feet (2.5 m) tall, and 10 wheeled

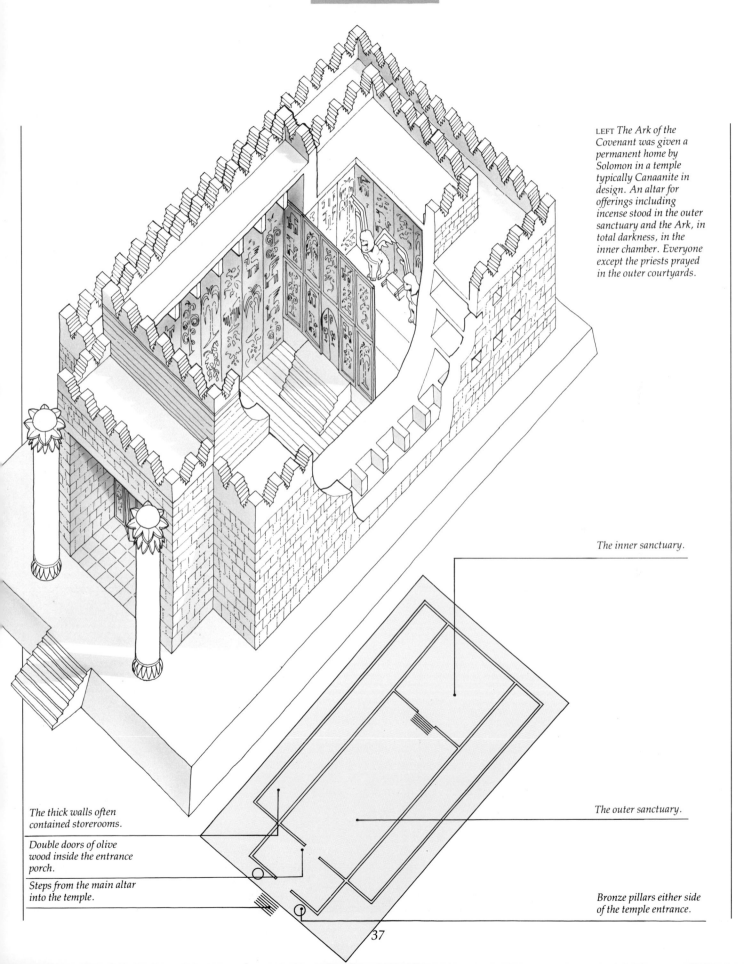

LEFT *The Ark of the Covenant was given a permanent home by Solomon in a temple typically Canaanite in design. An altar for offerings including incense stood in the outer sanctuary and the Ark, in total darkness, in the inner chamber. Everyone except the priests prayed in the outer courtyards.*

The inner sanctuary.

The outer sanctuary.

The thick walls often contained storerooms.

Double doors of olive wood inside the entrance porch.

Steps from the main altar into the temple.

Bronze pillars either side of the temple entrance.

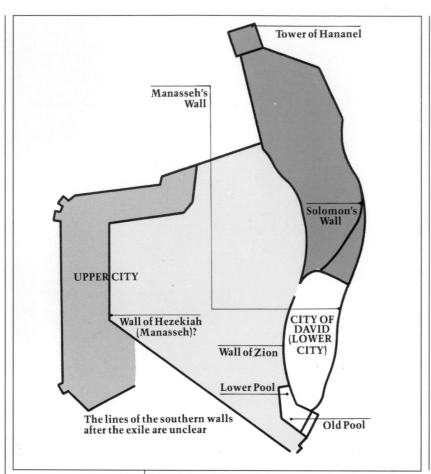

Tower of Hananel

Manasseh's
Wall

Solomon's
Wall

UPPER CITY

Wall of Hezekiah
(Manasseh)?

CITY OF
DAVID
(LOWER
CITY)

Wall of Zion

Lower Pool

Old Pool

**The lines of the southern walls
after the exile are unclear**

basins for carrying the water wherever it was needed in the Temple.

The architects of this first Hebrew Temple, and many of the workmen, were lent to King Solomon by the Canaanite King Hiram of Tyre, who also supplied the cedars for the pillars and the panelling. It survived for nearly 400 years, until the Babylonians destroyed it in 587 BC. Rebuilt by the Hebrews some 50 years later, after the Babylonian exile, the Temple was replaced magnificently by Herod the Great before and during the lifetime of Jesus, only to be destroyed during the Roman-Jewish War in AD 70. Since then it has never been replaced. Its site is now occupied by the oustandingly beautiful Moslem shrine, The Dome of the Rock.

A Golden Age

The Temple of Jerusalem and the royal palace were only some of the new buildings raised by King Solomon by the use of forced Hebrew labour. A number of Palestinian sites have the remains of massive fortifications constructed by Solomon, particularly Megiddo, Hazor and Gezer. The great shaft and tunnel at Megiddo, constructed to give safe access to the city's water supply in time of war, date from the time of Solomon or shortly after-

ABOVE *The original Canaanite city of Jerusalem before its conquest by David. The city sat on a narrow ridge and was quite easily defended. Solomon built the Temple to house the Ark in the northern flatter part of the city.*

LEFT *The cultivators of the fields. The period of peace secured by Kings David and Solomon became a golden age of Hebrew prosperity.*

wards, as do the massive casemate walls and gateway of the city.

Solomon established an efficient central administration with reliable written records. He developed a thriving foreign trade along the land routes and by using a merchant fleet based on the Red Sea. Excavations have also uncovered evidence of a large-scale copper industry based on ore deposits in the Jordan Valley and in the Negev area, south of the Dead Sea. The prosperity created by Solomon's administration gave rise to a golden age for the Hebrew people and established Solomon's reputation for 'wisdom'. Clearly, Solomon could not have succeeded without a deep understanding of the new opportunities the time offered his people, and the skill to overcome the divisive tendencies of traditional Hebrew tribal loyalties. It is a measure of Solomon's abilities that the national unity forged by him and his father, King David, collapsed at Solomon's death in 931 BC.

Civil War

With the death of King Solomon the united Hebrew kingdom split into two kingdoms, a southern one, Judah, with Jerusalem as its capital, and a northern kingdom, Israel, with Samaria as its eventual capital. The descendants of David continued to rule Judah in an unbroken line for three and a half centuries, while the bloody history of Israel is marked by frequent changes of dynasty until it was destroyed by the Assyrians in 721 BC.

Shortly after the split, Egypt reasserted her control over Palestines when the Pharaoh Sheshonk marched an army through the area and stripped the Temple of its main treasures as tribute. Both the Hebrew kingdoms continued to exist, but in mutual enmity. The northern Hebrews were always far more prosperous and numerous than their southern brethren, and this difference increased as the northern kingdom benefited from the trade routes which passed through it.

Golden Bulls

Differences in religious traditions added to contrasts in prosperity. Many Hebrews

RIGHT *Palestine was effectively at the nerve centre of a network of long-established trading routes and therefore ideally situated to take advantage of them once the Hebrews had overcome their enemies.*

——— Land routes

- - - Sea routes

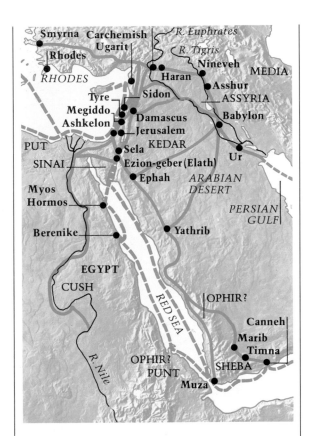

resented the change in emphasis exemplified by the new Temple in Jerusalem, especially as the old tribal priests had been replaced by the new line of priests appointed by the kings to the Temple. Ancient sanctuaries, such as Bethel, Shiloh, Shechem and Hebron, were overshadowed by Jerusalem.

The split between the kingdoms was sealed when the northern king, Jeroboam, declared that two of the old sanctuaries, Dan and Bethel, were now the official royal shrines of the northern kingdom. A golden bull was erected in each of them, and while this was a traditional symbol for the Hebrew God, Yahweh, it could easily be seen as a representation of the Canaanite god, Baal. The southern Hebrews denounced the northerners for supporting the Canaanite religion. There is evidence of the truth of this charge in the Bible's accounts of the struggle of such prophets as Elijah and Elisha against the Baal priests in the north. However, the southern Hebrews also encouraged the Canaanite religion up until the end of both kingdoms, and were denounced by such southern prophets as Isaiah and Jeremiah.

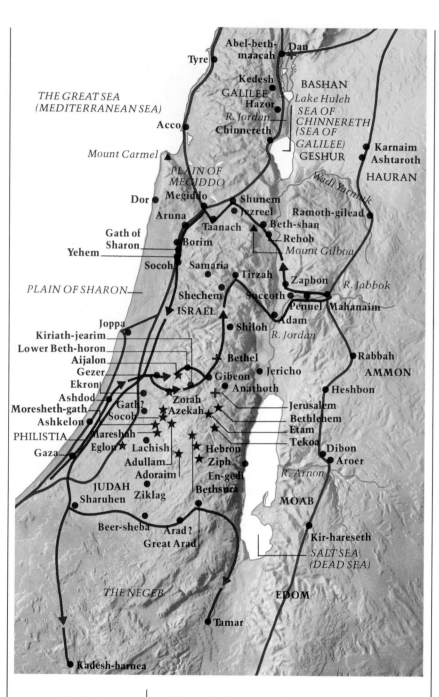

THE GREAT SEA
(MEDITERRANEAN SEA)

Tyre

Abel-beth-
maacah

Dan

Kedesh
GALILEE
Hazor

BASHAN

Lake Huleh
SEA OF
CHINNERETH
(SEA OF
GALILEE)

R. Jordan

Acco

Chinnereth

Karnaim
Ashtaroth

GESHUR

HAURAN

Mount Carmel

PLAIN OF
MEGIDDO

Wadi Yarmuk

Dor

Megiddo

Shunem
Jezreel

Ramoth-gilead

Aruna

Taanach

Beth-shan

Gath of
Sharon

Borim

Rehob
Mount Gilboa

Yehem

Socoh

Samaria

Tirzah

Zaphon

R. Jabbok

PLAIN OF SHARON

Shechem

Succoth

ISRAEL

Penuel Mahanaim

Joppa

Shiloh

Adam
R. Jordan

Kiriath-jearim

Lower Beth-horon

Bethel

Rabbah

Aijalon

Jericho

Gezer

Gibeon

AMMON

Ekron

Anathoth

Heshbon

Ashdod

Zorah

Gath?

Azekah

Jerusalem

Moresheth-gath

Socoh

Bethlehem

Ashkelon

Etam

PHILISTIA

Mareshah

Tekoa

Gaza

Eglon

Lachish

Hebron

Dibon

Adullam

Ziph

Aroer

Adoraim

En-gedi

R. Arnon

JUDAH

Bethsura

Sharuhen

Ziklag

MOAB

Beer-sheba

Arad?
Great Arad

Kir-hareseth

SALT SEA
(DEAD SEA)

THE NEGEB

EDOM

Tamar

Kadesh-barnea

RIGHT *Donkeys, the oldest
surviving beasts of
burden, are still used
today. The donkey was
ideally suited to the
climate of Palestine as it
could endure harsh
conditions and survive on
very coarse food.*

LEFT *Shortly after
Solomon's death, the
Egyptians, under
Sheshonk I, re-established
control of Palestine, taking
command of Jerusalem
and the trade routes.
Rehoboam, Solomon's
successor, quickly
alienated the northern
tribes by establishing his
power base in the south.
The northern kingdom,
which existed only for two
centuries, was by far the
more prosperous and
stronger of the two
kingdoms, but it was
crushed by the Assyrians
in 721 BC and its capital
was destroyed.*

— *Sheshank and the
Egyptian
campaign,
c 928 BC*

★ *King Rehoboam
of Judah's
fortresses*

+ *Royal sanctuaries*

— *Major trade
routes*

Egypt had regained control of the Palestinian coastal route to the north and to Mesopotamia, but her supremacy was short-lived.
During the eighth century BC Egypt was
once more torn by civil war, and the Assyrians of Mesopotamia had begun the great
expansion which would soon give them
possession of the Middle East from the Persian
Gulf to Upper Egypt.

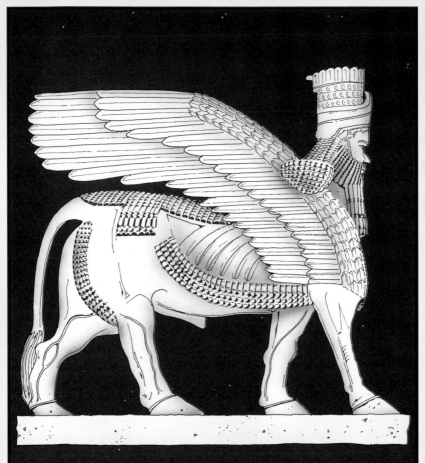

CHAPTER 3

New Terror

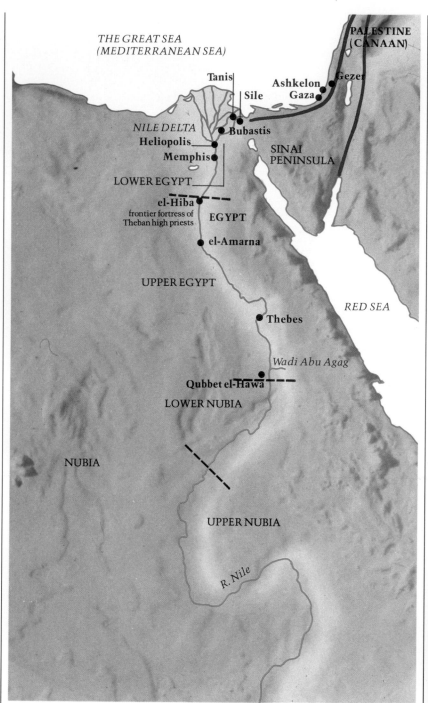

THE GREAT SEA
(MEDITERRANEAN SEA)

PALESTINE
(CANAAN)

Tanis

Ashkelon
Gaza
Gezer

Sile

NILE DELTA

Bubastis

Heliopolis

Memphis

LOWER EGYPT

SINAI
PENINSULA

el-Hiba
frontier fortress of
Theban high priests

EGYPT

el-Amarna

UPPER EGYPT

RED SEA

Thebes

Wadi Abu Agag

Qubbet el-Hawa

LOWER NUBIA

NUBIA

UPPER NUBIA

R. Nile

The Decline of Egypt

When the Hebrews escaped from Egypt to create a new nation in Palestine, Egypt was breaking into its two natural divisions, Upper and Lower Egypt. The attempted invasions by the 'Sea Peoples' (the Philistines) and the Libyans were stretching Egyptian defences to their limits. The Egyptians were in no position to prevent the Hebrews from penetrating into eastern Palestine, nor to stop the Philistines taking over the western coast.

Two centuries later, during the reigns of the Hebrew Kings David and Solomon, Lower Egypt was ruled from Tanis in the Nile delta where the coastal road leaves Egypt for Palestine and Mesopotamia. Theoretically, Upper Egypt was also ruled from Tanis, but

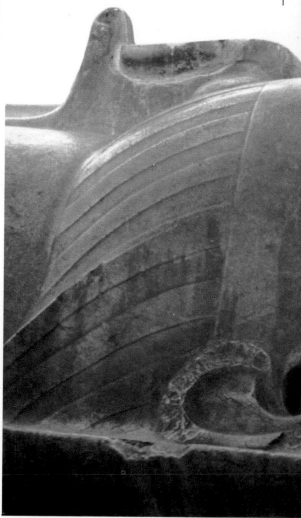

ABOVE *Such a long, narrow kingdom as Egypt soon split into warring factions if the central government was weak. The Tanis kings controlled the Nile delta area, but were only* *nominal sovereigns of Upper Egypt which was ruled by the Theban priests, who acknowledged the Tanis kings.*

- - - - Frontiers
———— Major trade routes

the priests of Thebes, the southern Egyptian capital, acted as an independent kingdom under the leadership of their hereditary high priest. The Tanis kings could only enforce their authority as far as the frontier fortress of el-Hiba, 60 miles (100 km) up the River Nile from Memphis.

Solomon's Temple Stripped

Egypt revived for a while under the first king of the next dynasty, a Libyan called Sheshonk, who was determined to regain full control of Palestine with its vital international routes. It was he who invaded the southern Hebrew kingdom of Judah and stripped the royal palace and the Temple of their treasures before returning to Egypt again.

BELOW *A fallen statue – a vivid symbol of a fallen dynasty in a divided Egypt.*

For a while Sheshonk managed to impose his rule over both parts of Egypt, but the unity was not to last. On his death, the country disintegrated once more into overlapping dynasties and areas ruled by independent cities with their own kings. The central Egyptian government could no longer assert any effective power. Soon, in the eighth century BC, the Assyrians would be rolling ruthlessly across the near east from Mesopotamia, through Palestine and into Egypt itself.

Egyptian royal tombs from this turbulent period have been excavated within the Temple area at Tanis, the capital of Lower Egypt. They reveal brick walls 30 feet (10 m) high and 45 feet (15 m) thick enclosing an area 500 yards (430 m) long by 400 yards (370 m) wide. Clearly, the uncertain times demanded that the temples should be turned into massive fortresses, where the state treasuries and the burial shrines of Egypt's divine kings could be safely guarded.

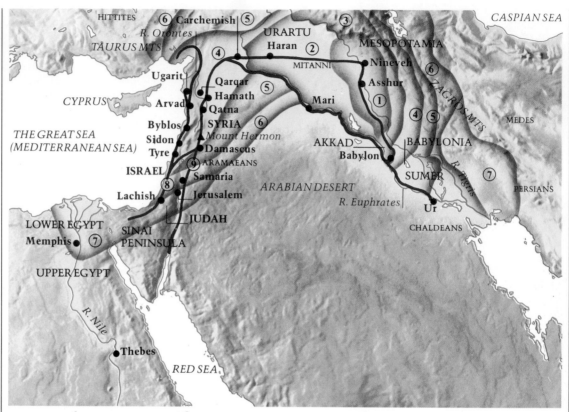

① *Nucleus of the Assyrian Empire*

② *Expansion in 14th century* BC

③ *Expansion in 13th century* BC

④ *Expansion in 9th century* BC

⑤ *Expansion during the reign of Tiglath-pileser III (745–727* BC)

⑥ *Expansion during reigns of Sargon II (721–705* BC) *and Sennacherib (704–681* BC)

⑦ *Expansion during reigns of Esarhaddon (680–669* BC) *and Ashurbanipal (668–630* BC)

—— *Major trade routes*

⑧ *The Way of the Sea*

⑨ *The King's Highway*

Anvil of the Powers

In the tenth century BC, not long after the death of the Hebrew King Solomon, a succession of Assyrian kings in Mesopotamia broke the power of their eastern enemies, subjugated the Babylonians to the south, and set about expanding Assyrian rule westwards towards the Great Sea. For a while the Assyrians were held in check by a coalition of 11 kings from Syria, Lebanon and Palestine, including the Hebrews, who defeated the Assyrians at the Battle of Qarqar on the River Orontes in 854 BC.

Soon, however, Assyrian patrols were probing into Palestine down the coastal road towards Egypt, and along the King's Highway on the eastern edge of the Jordan Valley. The Assyrians were not yet ready to occupy the region but the Palestinian kingdoms began to feel the pressure of Assyrian power. King Jehu of Israel, the northern Hebrew kingdom, bought off the Assyrian King Shalmaneser III with ingots of silver and gold, and vessels made of gold, but gained only a temporary respite for his people.

Assyria's Advance

New impetus was given to the Assyrian expansion by the most dynamic of its kings, Tiglath-pileser III, who crushed all opposition as his armies drove down through Palestine. Under Tiglath-pileser III and his successors, Assyria became the first power to create an empire stretching through the whole of the 'fertile crescent', from the Persian Gulf to Lower Egypt, with the international routes through Palestine as its main arteries. The two Hebrew kingdoms found themselves on opposite sides of the vital Assyrian lines of communication, and could not hope to retain their independence.

Tiglath-pileser III incorporated northern Palestine, including the Hebrew kingdom of Israel, into an Assyrian province, and exacted tribute from Judah, the southern Hebrew kingdom. Despite the fierce opposition of the prophet Isaiah, King Ahaz of Judah turned the small kingdom of Judah into an outpost of Assyrian power, and converted Solomon's great Temple into a shrine of the Assyrian religion to prove his loyalty to his new

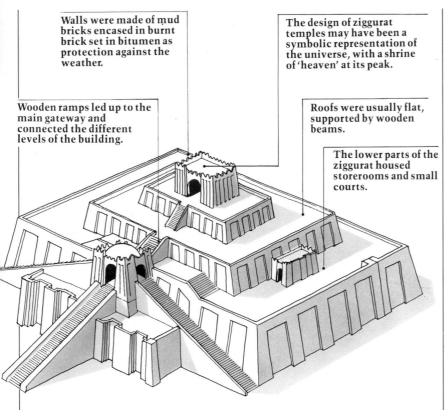

Walls were made of mud bricks encased in burnt brick set in bitumen as protection against the weather.

The design of ziggurat temples may have been a symbolic representation of the universe, with a shrine of 'heaven' at its peak.

Wooden ramps led up to the main gateway and connected the different levels of the building.

Roofs were usually flat, supported by wooden beams.

The lower parts of the ziggurat housed storerooms and small courts.

Assyria finally defeated the Egyptians early in the seventh century BC. However they did not manage to maintain effective control over their Egyptian possessions, for the empire was far too extended even for Assyrian armies. It collapsed quickly under the pressure of Scythian incursions from the east, and a rebellion by the Babylonians who captured the Assyrian capital, Nineveh in 612 BC and took over the empire.

The Assyrians worshiped a complex pantheon of 600 planetary and stellar deities, and 300 gods of the land of the dead. They also had a creation myth which included a tradition of a universal flood similar to the opening chapters of Genesis. The most dramatic remains of their religion are the great temple towers, the ziggurats, which have been unearthed from the upper reaches of the River Euphrates to the Persian Gulf.

The Babylonians

After the Babylonians had destroyed the Assyrian capital of Nineveh, they went on to defeat their other potential rival for power,

masters. It is hardly surprising that Isaiah's messianic prophecies date from this time: the Hebrews were desperately in need of a messiah who would bring them back to the covenant with God.

Deportations

The Assyrians completed the destruction of the northern Hebrew kingdom, Israel, and its capital Samaria, in 721 BC after a brief rebellion. The Hebrew population was deported (disappearing from history) and replaced with settlers from other parts of the empire. Twenty years later, rebellions erupted throughout the empire and the Palestinian states appealed to Egypt for help. An Egyptian army did march north but it was easily defeated by the Assyrians. King Hezekiah of Judah had seized the opportunity to reform his people's religion with the help of Isaiah, but the Assyrians besieged Jerusalem and accepted Hezekiah's submission after he had paid a crippling sum in tribute. There was to be no respite.

ABOVE *Ziggurats were built by the Mesopotamians to worship their astrology gods. Notable examples of ruined ziggurats are those at Ur and Khorsbad in Mesopotamia. These towering temples are an example of the energy and imagination of this ancient people, and a vivid expression of their religious beliefs.*

RIGHT *Like the Assyrians, the Babylonians worshipped a multitude of deities, some of which entered Hebrew folk traditions. This night demon is the model for 'Lilith' in the Hebrew stories.*

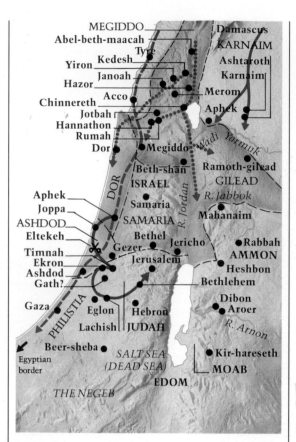

LEFT *The Hebrew kingdoms were subject to several military incursions when the Assyrians were led by Tiglath-pileser III. After advancing into Egypt along the coast, the Assyrians captured Damascus from the Syrians in 732 BC and exacted tribute. In 701 BC an operation was mounted against Judah. When Samaria was destroyed in 721 BC, Judah survived by becoming a puppet kingdom of the Assyrians. Hezekiah, King of Judah, was forced to pay tribute to the Assyrians, despite the support of Egypt.*

--- Route of Tiglath-pileser III in 734 BC

••••••• Route of Tiglath-pileser III in 733 BC

— Route of Tiglath-pileser III in 732 BC

Assyrian provinces

Expansion of Shalmaneser V and Sargon II, and provinces

— Route of Sennacherib's in 701 BC

✄ Defeat of Egyptian army, 701 BC

brief respite when an Egyptian army tried to relieve the city, the Babylonians finally destroyed it and deported king and people to Babylonia where the Hebrew monarchy ended. Palestine was lost to the Hebrews for 1the 48 years of their exile, until the Babylonians in their turn were overthrown by the Persians in 539 BC.

As a result of the exile, the city of Babylon became a symbol of oppression and corruption, instantly recognizable in the Bible by both Jews and Christians as typical of any powerful enemy. Situated on the river Euphrates near the south-eastern limits of Mesopotamia, the city and its people were far more tolerant than the Assyrians. It is significant that the exiled Hebrews in Babylonia retained their national identity and were able to use the exile period to give new meaning and vitality to their religion. The Babylonians' religion was a form of the beliefs predominant in Mesopotamia, with temple towers, a vast pantheon of gods, divination to discover the will of the gods and belief in a multitude of demons.

The Protest Movement

As the two Hebrew kingdoms came to terms with the new political and international scene after the death of King Solomon, the northern kingdom of Israel grew ever more prosperous from the great trading routes, by contrast with its southern neighbour, Judah. The weak control Egypt exercised over Palestine had little effect on the Hebrew kingdoms.

With prosperity came deep social stratification, stark inequality and injustice. The very shape of the towns changed as the wealthy Hebrews enlarged their houses at the expense of their poorer neighbours and forced them to crowd into the less attractive parts. Many people sold their land to meet their debts and slid inexorably into slavery. There was no redress for the poor in the corrupt courts of law.

The traditional Hebrew religion of the covenant insisted that the poor must be protected, and valued justice about all political virtues protected by divine law. This traditional religion still received recognition—with some adaptations to the newly acquired agricultural skills—in the ancient sanctuaries

the Egyptians, at Carchemish, on the borders of modern-day Syria and Turkey, and so gained control of Palestine. At first the Babylonians did little to trouble the only remaining Hebrew kingdom, Judah, and they allowed King Jehoiakim to continue ruling from his capital, Jerusalem. The Hebrews, however, once more appealed to the Egyptians to free them from foreign rule, and when the Babylonians heard of this they attacked Jerusalem and captured it after a three month siege.

Jerusalem Destroyed

The Hebrew king and his leading officials were all deported to Babylon, where they were allowed to live at Babylonian expense in some comfort. However, the new Hebrew government in Jerusalem continued intrigues with Egypt, despite the opposition of the prophet Jeremiah, and in 589 BC the Babylonians again attacked Jerusalem. This time the siege lasted nearly three years. Despite a

of Palestine, such as Beer-sheba, Hebron, Bethel, Shiloh, Shechem, Dan, Mount Carmel, Mount Ebal, Mount Gerizim and Mount Hermon. In addition, there was the new Temple built by King Solomon in Jerusalem to house the main symbol of the Hebrew religion and its sacred law: the Ark of the Covenant. However, many Hebrews had adopted the native Canaanite religion of Baal, with its law of might, its worship of the fertility gods and goddesses, human sacrifice and sacred prostitution at the 'high places'. In such a religion the poor and weak had no rights.

Fearless Teachers

In this situation a new group of religious leaders emerged, the prophets. They were fearless popular teachers, independent of the royal courts and official sanctuaries. They were prepared to denounce kings, priests and judges as they stole their subjects' lands,

ABOVE *Vines growing near Lachish. In their teaching, the prophets promised prosperity, symbolized by vines, for obedience to God, and the catastrophes like the Assyrian destruction of Lachish for disobedience.*

gave official recognition to the Baal religion, and maintained their power ruthlessly by torture and murder. Often, the prophets paid for their courage with their lives.

The first of the prophets to leave a book of his teachings was Amos, a shepherd from the south who denounced the northern kings and their administration at the royal sanctuary of Bethel. A little later, Hosea continued Amos's work, and taught that the Hebrew God of the covenant, Yahweh, was the real source of his people's prosperity, not the Canaanite fertility gods. Hosea opened the way for a new, less legalistic understanding of the covenant with God by teaching that he is a forgiving God, whose tender, steadfast love will always save the Hebrews.

Israel Destroyed

The most famous prophet at this time was Isaiah, who taught in the southern Hebrew kingdom, Judah, at the time when the

Assyrians began their drive southwards into Palestine to secure their frontiers with Egypt. King Ahaz of Jerusalem saw that the Assyrians were too powerful to be stopped, so he seized the opportunity to become an ally of the Assyrians and adopted the Assyrian religion to prove his loyalty. Despite Isaiah's protests, Ahaz replaced the traditional Hebrew religion with Assyrian worship in the Temple in Jerusalem and made Judah an Assyrian base. Isaiah tried to stop Ahaz with the famous 'Immanuel' warning (Isa 7:14), and when he was ignored went on to teach that God would save his people with a faithful and just king, a 'messiah'.

Backed by Judah, the Assyrians destroyed the northern Hebrew kingdom, Israel, in 721 BC, deported its people and replaced them with groups from other parts of the Assyrian empire. The capital of Israel was Samaria, and in these groups of incomers who settled in Samaria and its district we can see the first beginnings of the 'Samaritans' so hated by

ABOVE *Jews with a scroll. The scrolls of the sacred Hebrew writings included the teachings of the prophets, who were often more influential through their writings, after their death, than their preaching during their lifetime.*

the southern Jews in New Testament times. Despite a brief rebellion by King Ahaz's successor, Hezekiah, which the Assyrians suppressed, Judah and Jerusalem survived intact, but only as a firm ally of the Assyrians.

Caught in the age-old dilemma of small nations trying to survive when the great international powers fought each other across small nations' lands, each of the Hebrew kingdoms was eventually destroyed. Israel, the northern kingdom was wiped out by the Assyrians early in their occupation of Palestine and its people were deported never to return. (Since then, various people have claimed to be 'the lost tribes of Israel', including British and American groups.) Judah, the southern kingdom, managed to survive for the remaining hundred years of the Assyrians, only to fall to the Babylonians. The people of Judah eventually emerged again after nearly 50 years of exile in Babylonia, and rebuilt their nation to become the 'Jews', but it was a miraculous survival.

Preserving the Traditions

Throughout the long years of turmoil, and political and religious compromise, a succession of great prophets fought to keep the Hebrew people faithful to the God of the covenant: Elijah, Elisha, Amos, Hosea, Isaiah, Micah, Jeremiah, Habbakuk and Ezekiel, to name but some of them. Although they failed to influence political events, they did help keep alive the main features of the Hebrew religion and in particular the vital importance of justice and righteousness as expressions of God's rule and love.

Other forces also helped preserve the nation's religious traditions. Despite its use by 'foreign' priests and religions, the great Temple in Jerusalem remained a visible reminder of the escape from Egypt and the covenant while the Ark of the Covenant was enshrined in its innermost sanctuary. The psalms preserved the essential beliefs of the

ABOVE *The Western Wall of the Temple in Jerusalem. Even now, the foundations of the great platform on which the Temple stood are the focus for keeping alive Hebrew traditions. In his reforms, King Josiah made the Temple the only national centre for the Hebrew religion.*

Hebrew faith as popular songs, as also did the collections of folk wisdom found in such books of the Bible as Proverbs and Ecclesiasticus.

Above all, the central principles of Hebrew law were still preserved, no matter how corrupt the courts might have become as they administered it, for there was no real distinction between the religious and the secular in everyday life. All actions and transactions came within the sphere of religion, as the Bible shows, and this could still be the traditional Hebrew religion if only it had the support of the nation's leaders.

The Great Reform

Hebrew religious insights were never fixed and unchangeable, but developed steadily as the people coped with life, first under Assyrian occupation, then under the Babylonians—including the long years of exile—and on into the Persian period. Towards the end of the seventh century BC the Hebrews of Judah suddenly found themselves free from foreign occupation for a brief 15 years. They seized the opportunity to make sweeping reforms and to dedicate the nation to God again.

The long reign of Manasseh of Judah (687–642 BC) was a disaster for his people with religious chaos and complete subjection to the Assyrians. Manasseh practised human sacrifice at the terrible Molech shrine just outside Jerusalem. The Temple itself was made a centre for the Assyrian astrological worship of the plants and stars, and the sacred prostitution of the Canaanite fertility religion. The example of Jerusalem was imitated throughout the country and no one dared to protest.

Then quite suddenly the overstretched Assyrian empire disintegrated. Egypt broke away, and at the other end of the empire in Mesopotamia the Babylonians rebelled. Hordes of Scythians swept into Mesopotamia from the eastern mountain ranges and forced the Assyrians to withdraw their troops from Palestine to protect their homelands. They never returned.

Enforcing the Law

King Josiah of Judah (640–609 BC), supported by the young prophet Jeremiah, seized the chance to repair the Temple in Jerusalem as the Assyrians withdrew, and to establish the supremacy of the traditional Hebrew religion again. Soon after the work on the Temple had begun, masons working on the walls found a large scroll hidden in the stonework. It proved to be the full codification of Hebrew law, and occupies most of the biblical Book of Deuteronomy. It showed how Hebrew law applies the central insights of the covenant with God to every detail of daily life, and gives clear, practical rules for the whole range of religious and secular activities in a society, from worship to town planning.

Josiah set out to enforce the laws of Deuteronomy in his kingdom and in the former kingdom of Israel. He removed all traces of the Baal cult and the Assyrian religion from the Temple and from the 'high

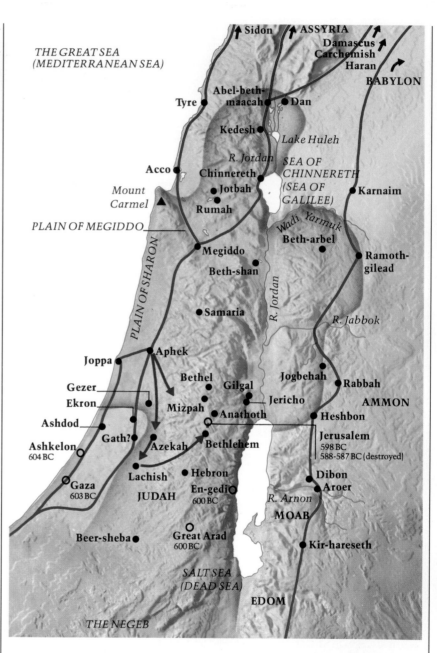

places', and destroyed the shrine of Molech outside the southern walls of Jerusalem where children were sacrificed. From now onwards (and still so today), the Temple in Jerusalem was to be the only place in the world where the main sacrificial rites of the Hebrew religion could be performed legally, under the strict supervision of the official priests. It was this regulation which made Jerusalem the centre of pilgrimage for Jews throughout the world.

Josiah of Jerusalem's Kingdom (640–609 BC)

○ Conquest of Palestine by Nebuchadnezzar and the Babylonians (605–562 BC)

—— Jerusalem and the final campaign (588–587 BC)

—— Major trade routes

ABOVE *The ruins in the older part of Jerusalem have been excavated and confirm the deliberate destruction of the city in 587 BC.*

LEFT *The Babylonians turned their attention to the 'fertile crescent' after vanquishing the Assyrians in Mesopotamia. At the same time King Josiah was introducing his religious reforms, destroying the shrines of foreign religions, and giving new life to the old Hebrew laws of the covenant. Under Nebuchadnezzar the invaders were a much stronger and more unified force; they captured important towns including Jerusalem which they took in 598 BC and then destroyed almost 10 years later.*

The King's Mistake

Carried away by the success of his reform, King Josiah of Judah thought that God would keep his kingdom safe from foreign interference. It was a fatal mistake. The Egyptian King Necho II marched an army through Palestine in 609 BC to support the Assyrians in their final struggle against the Babylonians, in an attempt to maintain the balance of power in the Near and Middle East. The Egyptians failed and Babylonia rose to supremacy, but it ended the brief spell of freedom for the Hebrews, as Josiah tried to oppose the passage of the Egyptian army and was killed at the battle of Megiddo.

Josiah's death in 609 BC was the beginning of the end for the Hebrew kingdom of Judah, and for the line of kings directly descended from King David. Egypt took control of Palestine again, but only for four years until

the Babylonians destroyed the last Assyrian army in 605 BC. Later that same year the Babylonian king, Nebuchadnezzar, drove southwards through Palestine to attack the Egyptians. The Babylonians were repulsed by the Egyptians with heavy losses, but Nebuchadnezzar kept hold of Palestine and King Jehoiakim of Judah submitted his kingdom and his people to him.

The First Exiles

After the long years of Assyrian domination, the Hebrews of Judah expected the Babylonians to be as ruthless as the power they had overthrown. Both the king and people hoped that Egypt would regain control of Palestine so that they could benefit from the milder rule of Egypt. King Jehoiakim stopped the tribute payments to the Babylonians,

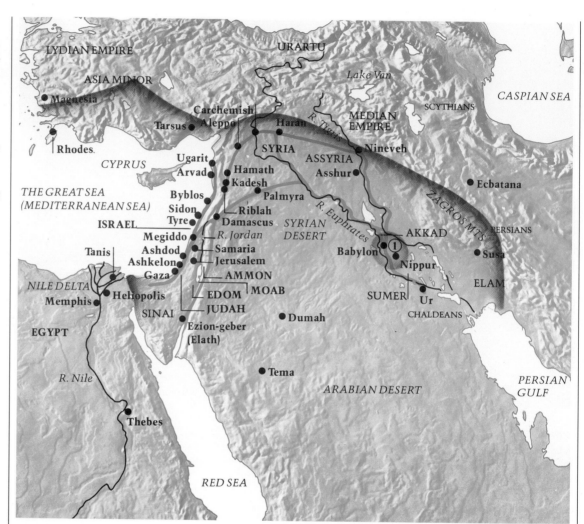

RIGHT *The Hebrews were deported to Babylon after the destruction of Jerusalem in 587 BC. The destruction came after a two year siege; it was the second time that the Babylonians had been forced to subdue the city in less than 10 years. The Hebrews remained in exile until the overthrow of Babylon by Persia almost 50 years later. During the years of exile the Hebrews came to regard the destruction of Jerusalem and their deportation as a process of purification. It was an opportunity to reform the nation before they were allowed to return to Jerusalem.*

Limits of
Babylonian
Empire

Major trade
routes

① Probable site
of exile

called for Egyptian help and trusted to the strength of Jerusalem and an Egyptian victory over the Babylonians.

He died before he could learn how mistaken he was, for it was his son, Jehoiachin, who surrendered Jerusalem to the Babylonians after a siege of three months in 598 BC. The Babylonians were remarkably lenient to the Hebrew people and their leaders, perhaps because they had been spared taking Jerusalem by assault. King Jehoiachin and his court were taken to a comfortable captivity in Babylon from which they expected to be released at any moment, despite the repeated warnings of such prophets as Jeremiah and Ezekiel. Although Jerusalem was not yet destroyed, this was the beginning of the long exile of the Hebrew people in Babylonia, which was to have such deep effects on the

Hebrews' understanding of their religion and on the Bible. Through his visions of God manifesting himself in Babylonia, Ezekiel realized that God had deserted Jerusalem and the Temple and was now with the exiles in Babylonia, but Ezekiel could not convince the exiles or the Hebrews of Jerusalem. They would not be convinced until Jerusalem was destroyed.

Destruction of Jerusalem

The new Hebrew king in Jerusalem, Zedekiah, foolishly thought that Babylonian leniency was a sign of weakness and called again for Egyptian help to support a Hebrew rebellion. This time Jerusalem resisted the inevitable

Babylonian siege for nearly three years and when it was finally taken in 587 BC the Babylonians destroyed it. Zedekiah's two sons were executed before him and Zedekiah taken in chains to Babylon together with the bulk of the people. The kingdom of Judah was finished, all its cities in ruins and only the poorest of its people, left scattered, remained. Although the Hebrews would retain their identity in Babylonia, and would never forget the glory of David and Solomon when they were the undisputed masters of Palestine, it would be 48 years before the Hebrew exiles could return to build their capital and their nation.

The Exile in Babylonia

The long exile in Babylonia from 587 to 539 BC deprived the Hebrews of most of the visible symbols of their covenant religion. The Temple of Jerusalem and the Ark of the Covenant were destroyed, and this had been the only place where they could offer the sacrifices of animals and crops central to their worship. The long line of Davidic kings ends with the Babylonian exile and the destruction of David's capital, Jerusalem. These kings had been the visible guardians of God's covenant, no matter how they had failed. However, the most powerful covenant symbol of all was Palestine itself, the Holy Land, promised to them by God, and the exiles were separated from it apparently indefinitely.

The exiles had in fact taken with them other symbols of their religion as powerful as the ones they had lost, had they but known it. These were their historical traditions, which recorded in oral form no less than in writing how God had made himself known to the people's ancestors, in the escape from Egypt, and in the triumphs of David. They also had their legal traditions, formulated as expressions of the covenant, and their memories of the sacred rituals of the Temple of Jerusalem, including the hymns and music they used in their worship and which they could still sing in Babylonia. The Hebrew priests became the guardians of the nation's traditions now that they could no longer preside over the sacrifices. This ensured that the Hebrew

RIGHT *On the River Euphrates, a little way to the south of modern Baghdad stood the ancient city of Babylon. From here the rulers of Babylon controlled the whole of southern Mesopotamia. Babylon was defended by a double wall with eight gates, and straddled the river Euphrates. The old city was connected to its new extensions by two bridges. The city was divided into sections by great avenues and there was also a network of canals. The city was built of hard baked mud bricks with imaginative relief sculptures reflecting the impressive architecture. Babylon was the centre of the empire in the second millenium BC. It later fell into decline and became an Assyrian province. However, the Babylonians rebelled in 626 BC and eventually overthrew the Assyrian Empire in 612 BC.*

ABOVE *The main entrance into Babylon was through the Ishtar Gate. The gate itself was covered with blue enamelled brick reliefs of bulls and dragons. The adjacent buildings had friezes of lions on their walls. In the New Year festival, a statue of Marduk, the chief god of Babylon, was carried in procession along an avenue and through the Ishtar Gate. The great avenue stretched right across the city and was paved with pink marble and limestone.*

LEFT *The god Marduk's temple was an enormous brick structure, known as the Tower of Babel. It was 300 feet (90 metres) square and 300 feet (90 metres) high, and shaped like a pyramid. An outer staircase led to the upper levels with a shrine at their apex.*

ABOVE *One of the seven wonders of the ancient world – the legendary 'hanging gardens' of Babylon. They were built on the roof of the royal palace of King Nebuchadnezzar*

ABOVE *The great statue of the chief god of Babylon, was housed in the temple of Marduk (4) which was part of a sacred complex that included the ziggurat temple (5). During the time of Nebuchadnezzar a whole new district (3) was added, across the River Euphrates (2), as the population grew in size. Nebuchadnezzar also added a further wall (8), to the south of the ancient* walls, *to strengthen the defences. The main temple area was reached by a processional way which led from the Ishtar Gate (9). Cutting diagonally across the city was the canal (6), which was part of the defences. There were other canals that helped to control the flooding. Outside the city lay the main burial place (1) and the theatre (7)*

RIGHT *The main sport of kings in Mesopotamia was lion hunting as the animals were so numerous. Used as symbols of royal power and courage, lions were a favourite feature of decoration, particularly to flank processional routes, as in Babylon.*

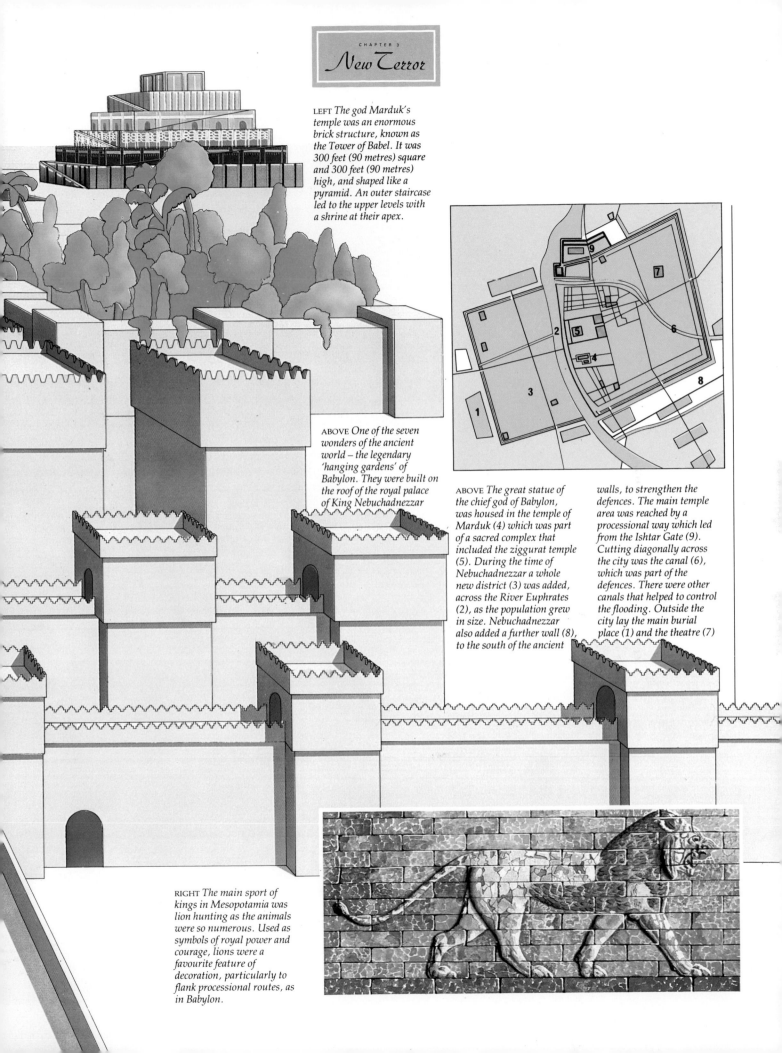

RIGHT *The tasks of working the land and winning food from it are no less arduous in Israel today than they were in ancient Palestine, and the technology used is not always that different.*

LEFT *Oranges, fruit of the same creative power of God that produced abundant harvests and convinced the Hebrews that their covenant with him would last forever.*

people did not lose their identity by being absorbed into the religion and culture of Babylon. The priests replaced the kings as the leaders of the Hebrew community, together with such charismatic teachers as Ezekiel and anonymous Hebrew prophets.

The Nation's Heritage

Consequently, the exiles were able to reflect on the nation's history, and rewrite their records and traditions to show the religious patterns running through it all. Most of the history books in the Old Testament were written during the exile, under the influence of the Book of Deuteronomy. The key principle they discovered was obedience: if the people were faithful to the covenant with God and to the laws which applied it to everyday life, they prospered. If they were disobedient, they would be punished to purify them and to bring them back to God

again. Above all, they must protect the traditions of worship evolved in the Temple in Jerusalem so that they could restore them, when the opportunity arose, in all their purity.

Surrounded by the magnificence of the Babylonian civilization and its religion, the Hebrews in exile turned to their own history for evidence that their God really was all-powerful and even showed his power through his people's misfortunes. God was using the Babylonians to purify his people. This theme was further developed by the Temple priests in exile as they collected together the traditions of their nation and wove them into a teaching pattern which would demonstrate the supreme power of God. The resulting account was the collection of writings which form the opening five books of the Old Testament: Genesis, Exodus, Leviticus, Numbers and Deuteronomy.

God's Creative Power

The materials used by the priests for their record of the fundamentals of Hebrew religion were the traditional stories about the creation of the universe; the accounts of the first human beings, of the flood, and of the Tower of Babel; the history of the patriarchs and their immediate descendants, of the Hebrews in Egypt and their escape, their covenant with God and journey through the wilderness; and the great collections of Hebrew law. All this material was then arranged within a narrative framework which demonstrated how God's creative power was at work throughout the events and in all the laws. The opening chapter of the Book of Genesis (1:1–2:4) is the priestly author's introduction to the whole work, to show an ideal world which God still intends to restore with mankind as the administrator of his plan.

This view of history gave the Hebrews confidence in the future, and inspired them to tackle the work of reconstruction when they returned to the ruined Jerusalem after the exile ended. In this view of history we can detect the influence of such prophets as Jeremiah and Ezekiel, who promised the exiles a new covenant in which God would transform his people and make it possible for them to obey him and respond to his will.

CHAPTER 4

Rebuilding the Nation

The Return

The main shape of the Old Testament as we now know it was forged in the suffering of the Babylonian exile between the years 587 and 539 BC. It would all have been in vain if the Hebrew people had not been able to rebuild their nation when they were allowed to return to Palestine. That return was made possible by the enlightened generosity of one of history's greatest soldiers and statesmen, King Cyrus of Persia.

Cyrus received the surrender of Babylon in 539 BC when his armies were still a distance from the city, after a lightning campaign in which the Persian forces had swept across the eastern frontiers of the Babylonian empire from the Indian Ocean to the Black Sea, and then southwards into the heart of Mesopotamia to Babylon itself. By 538 BC Cyrus was ruler of the whole of Babylon's former empire, including Palestine and the descendants of the Hebrew exiles who were taken from Judah and Jerusalem to Babylonia in 598 and 587 BC. The Persian king decreed that exiles could return to their homelands with their return financed from Persian funds, carrying the treasures looted from them by the Babylonians.

Enough Jews (as they may now be called) returned to Palestine to make a fresh start in Jerusalem, but many remained in Mesopotamia as the beginnings of the Jewish 'diaspora', those Jews outside Palestine who from now onwards would always be far more numerous than the Jews of the Holy Land. After such a display of generosity by the Persians, it is not surprising that the Bible sees the hand of God in Cyrus's victories (Isa 40–55).

Rule by Priests

If the Persians intended that the new Jewish community in Jerusalem should be ruled by their old line of Davidic kings the plans came to nothing, as it was the priests of the Temple (or their descendants) who led the returned exiles. Even before the foundations of the new Temple had been laid, the priests restored the sacrificial worship practised on the site before the exile.

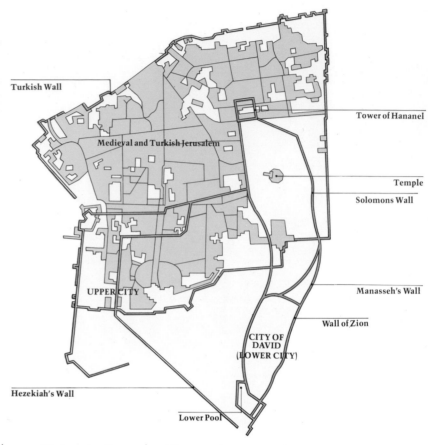

Turkish Wall

Medieval and Turkish Jerusalem

Tower of Hananel

Temple

Solomons Wall

UPPER CITY

Manasseh's Wall

Wall of Zion

CITY OF DAVID (LOWER CITY)

Hezekiah's Wall

Lower Pool

ABOVE *The Jerusalem the Hebrew exiles returned to from Babylon was in ruins, a shadow of its former self. The city was rebuilt only gradually following similar plans to those of David's earlier city and those of Hezekiah and Manasseh. Near the end of the Old Testament period, Jerusalem ran from the Hinnom valley in the west to the Kidron valley in the east.*

The newly returned Jews then made a diplomatic blunder which was to have far reaching effects for their troubled future. The Samaritans, who occupied the area north of Jerusalem which had once been the Hebrew kingdom of Israel, asked to help with the rebuilding of the Temple, and when their help was curtly refused they began to hinder the work. A series of poor harvests added to the troubles of the returned exiles and they felt that they had best devote their efforts to building houses and growing food, rather than restoring the Temple. It was more than 20 years before the new Temple was completed and dedicated.

The New Jerusalem

Until Jerusalem and its Temple was rebuilt and secure, the new Jewish community had no chance of survival against its many traditional enemies. Two men, Nehemiah and Ezra (whose names are attached to books of the Bible) eventually saved the new

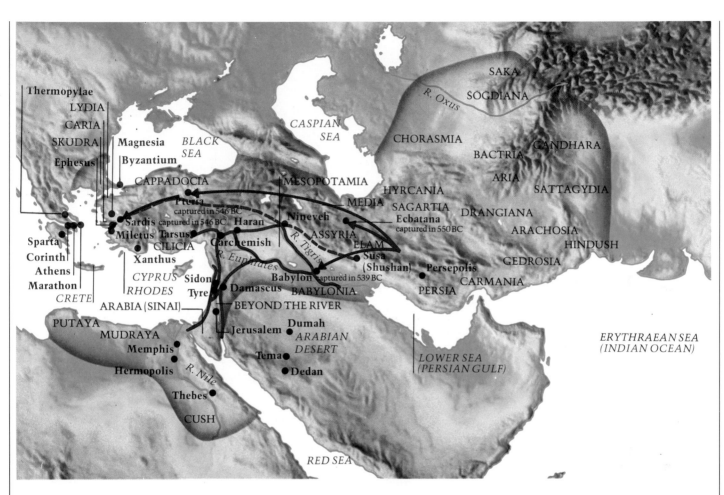

The following map labels appear on the illustration:

SAKA, SOGDIANA, R. Oxus, CHORASMIA, BACTRIA, GANDHARA, ARIA, SATTAGYDIA, HYRCANIA, SAGARTIA, DRANGIANA, ARACHOSIA, HINDUSH, ECBATANA captured in 550 BC, MEDIA, GEDROSIA, CARMANIA, Persepolis, PERSIA, Susa (Shushan), ELAM, ASSYRIA, Nineveh, MESOPOTAMIA, R. Tigris, R. Euphrates, Babylon captured in 539 BC, BABYLONIA, BEYOND THE RIVER, CASPIAN SEA, BLACK SEA, CAPPADOCIA, Pteria captured in 546 BC, Sardis captured in 546 BC, Haran, Carchemish, Tarsus, CILICIA, Miletus, Xanthus, Ephesus, Byzantium, Magnesia, SKUDRA, CARIA, LYDIA, Thermopylae, Sparta, Corinth, Athens, Marathon, CRETE, CYPRUS, RHODES, Sidon, Tyre, Damascus, ARABIA (SINAI), Jerusalem, Dumah, ARABIAN DESERT, Tema, Dedan, PUTAYA, MUDRAYA, Memphis, Hermopolis, R. Nile, Thebes, CUSH, RED SEA, LOWER SEA (PERSIAN GULF), ERYTHRAEAN SEA (INDIAN OCEAN)

community as it struggled to rebuild and consolidate.

Nehemiah was a Jew in a position of authority in the Persian royal court who visited Jerusalem and encouraged its citizens to finish the rebuilding of the city walls. He then served as governor for 12 years and made Jerusalem a city which would attract more Jews from Persia and Babylonia to return to it. To secure greater loyalty to the traditional Hebrew religion, Nehemiah also legislated against mixed marriages between Jews and non-Jews.

What Nehemiah started was taken even further by Ezra, who arrived in Jerusalem in 398 BC from the Babylonian Jewish community, armed with the Persian royal authority to give the Jews of Jerusalem an official law by which they must live. This he provided in the form of the first five books of the Old Testament, which contain the whole body of Jewish religious, civil and criminal law.

ABOVE *Cyrus extended the frontiers of the Persian empire westwards through Mesopotamia and Asia Minor during the 6th century BC, an expansion given greater impetus still and consolidated by his successors Cambyses II and Darius I. The Persians were defeated decisively by the Greeks at Marathon in 490 BC, although their empire survived for some 200 years.*

Campaigns of Cyprus

These books also record the saving acts of God in the creation of the universe, the escape from Egypt and the covenant God made with the Jews' ancestors. The saving acts of divine love are the real basis of the law.

Ezra went beyond Nehemiah's regulations against mixed marriages by forcing Jewish men who had married non-Jewish women to divorce their wives and renounce any children of the marriage, a law which helped provide the basis for the exclusiveness of the Jewish religion.

The Last Days of Persia

The Persian empire lasted for more than 200 years, and at its height the Persian kings ruled from the north-west of the Indus Valley in India to Asia Minor, and from the Persian

RIGHT *Corinth was an important commercial and strategic city even before Alexander the Great's time. In 27 BC it became the Roman governor's seat for the administration of all of Greece south of Macedonia. Corinth's cosmopolitan population offered a real challenge to Paul when he travelled there in AD 50 to spread the message of Christianity.*

Gulf to Egypt (where the Persian emperors constituted themselves in the 27th Dynasty of Egyptian pharaohs). Control of Egypt was never easy, however, with the Persian capital so far away at Ecbatana, particularly after the Persians were defeated by the Greeks at Marathon in 490 BC. They lost control of Egypt for nearly 60 years, and regained it for only 10 years before the whole empire fell to Alexander the Great.

The Persians organized their empire in provinces administered by 'satraps', officials who were given a large measure of independent authority by the central government. Effective control was maintained by the emperors ' through a system of separate military commands and an efficient system of royal couriers unsurpassed in the ancient world until the Romans linked their empire's provinces with a massive network of roads.

The official language of the Persian empire,

ABOVE *The substantial ruins at Persepolis bear silent witness to its greatness in Darius I's time before its destruction by Alexander the Great.*

Aramaic, became the everyday language of Palestine which Jesus and the disciples spoke. The main Persian religion was Zoroastrianism, a monotheism which viewed the universe as a battleground between good and evil, and worshipped Ahura Mazda, the creator, lawgiver and god of light.

The Greek Influence

Despite the fact that the Persians were so tolerant towards their Jewish subjects, it was the Greeks who left the deepest mark on them. The whirlwind campaigns of Alexander the Great, which delivered the Persian empire into his hands between 336 and his death in 323 BC, ensured that the Greek way of life would predominate from Greece itself to the western parts of India.

RIGHT *The walls of Jerusalem, without which the city would never have survived.*

MACEDONIA

HELLESPONT

Byzantium

AEGEAN SEA

Abydos

MYSIA

Mytilene

Thermopylae

Plataea

Thebes

LYDIA

IONIA

Marathon

Ephesus

Corinth
Athens

Miletus

Sparta

COS

NAXOS

RHODES

LEFT *The Greek colonies in coastal Asia Minor attempted, unsuccessfully, to assert their independence from their Persian masters – a move that provoked the Persians into attacking mainland Greece itself. The Persians took Athens in 480 BC, but were themselves eventually forced to withdraw by the Greeks.*

Persian routes:
—— *Fleet and army 492 BC*
– – *Fleet 490 BC*
- - - *Fleet 480 BC*
····· *Army 480 BC*

Hem

Mai

ABOVE *The Greeks were natural sailors and traders and founded trading communities throughout the Mediterranean region. Greek influence and culture spread far overland from these points.*

▬▬ *Areas of coast with numerous Greek colonies*

◉ *Mother cities*

● *Colonial cities*

Region of the Ionian revolt (500–494 BC)

Until Alexander's meteoric rise to power as king of Macedonia at the age of 20, Greece had been a country of independent city-states linked by a common language, culture and religion. By the time the Hebrews went into captivity in Babylonia, two and a half centuries before Alexander, the Greeks had already established colonies throughout the Mediterranean region, from what is now Rostov where the River Don flows into the Black Sea east of the Crimea, to Mainake (Malaga) in Spain. The Greek colonies were clustered most thickly around the foot of Italy and Sicily, and in the Black Sea. The real heartland of 'Greater Greece' was in the Aegean area, from mainland Greece to the western coast of Asia Minor. Undoubtedly, the Hebrews came under Greek influence long before the time of Alexander.

Persia and Greece

As the Persians extended their empire from the Indian Ocean to the shores of the Mediterranean, they could not resist the temptation to extend their rule even further westwards into Europe by invading Macedonia and the Greek peninsula. It was the most serious threat the Greek states ever encountered before the expansion of Rome, and for a brief period the Greeks ignored their internal enmities to unite against the invading Persians.

In a series of famous battles in the fifth century BC, which included Marathon, Thermopylae, Salamis and Plataeae, the Greeks repelled the Persians and forced them back into Asia Minor. The co-operation between the Greek states was short-lived, and by the end of the fifth century BC they were again locked in bitter civil war. Yet during the years of interstate strife, Greece still created a culture which influenced the ancient and modern world far more than any other has done, and certainly more permanently than any of the great military powers. It was expressed in a wide range of media: architecture, sculpture, drama, historical writings, poetry, philosophy and political theory, which had an immediate impact on all who came into contact with them.

Alexander the Great

The conquests of Alexander ensured that the cultural influence of the Greeks would be felt throughout the ancient world. He swiftly established the supremacy of his native

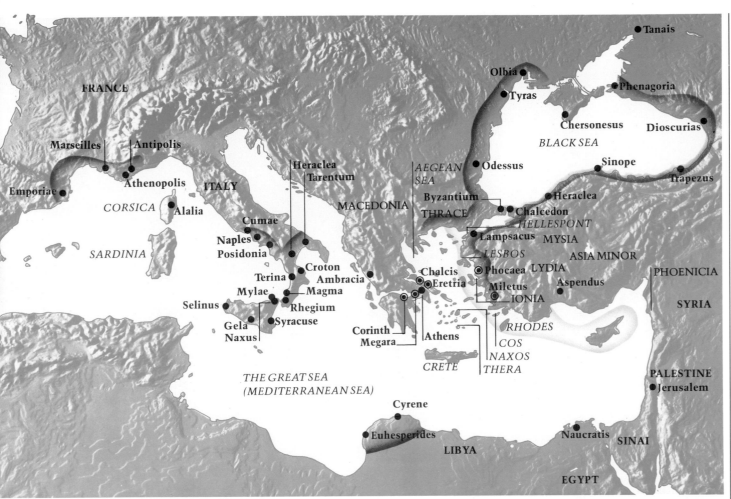

FRANCE

Marseilles
Antipolis
Emporiae
Athenopolis
ITALY
CORSICA
Alalia
Cumae
Naples
Posidonia
SARDINIA
Croton
Terina
Ambracia
Mylae
Magma
Selinus
Rhegium
Gela
Syracuse
Naxos

Heraclea
Tarentum
MACEDONIA

Chalcis
Eretria

Corinth
Megara
Athens

THE GREAT SEA
(MEDITERRANEAN SEA)

CRETE

AEGEAN
SEA
THRACE
Byzantium
Chalcedon
HELLESPONT
Lampsacus
MYSIA
LESBOS
ASIA MINOR
Phocaea
LYDIA
Miletus
Aspendus
IONIA

RHODES
COS
NAXOS
THERA

Tanais

Olbia
Tyras
Phenagoria

Chersonesus
Dioscurias
BLACK SEA

Odessus
Sinope
Trapezus

Heraclea

PHOENICIA

SYRIA

PALESTINE
Jerusalem

Cyrene
Euhesperides
LIBYA
Naucratis
SINAI

EGYPT

Macedonia and united the other Greek states under his rule by destroying Thebes. Then in 334 BC Alexander crossed the Hellespont into Asia Minor with a Greek army to liberate the Greek states of Ionia from Persian rule.

It was soon clear that there could be no security for Greater Greece until the Persian King Darius III had been defeated, and this Alexander achieved in 333 BC at Issus on the borders of Asia Minor and Syria. The victory opened the way through Syria, Phoenicia and Palestine to Egypt, and almost every-where Alexander was welcomed as a liberator. In Egypt he founded the port of Alexandria and had his personal divinity confirmed by the oracle of Zeus at the Siwa oasis in the Sahara desert.

By the winter of 331 BC, Alexander had defeated the remnants of Persian opposition, passed through Babylon and Susa in Meso-

RIGHT *Sheep were domesticated particularly early in Mesopotamia for their meat, milk, wool and possibly because they were one of the preferred animals for sacrifice.*

69

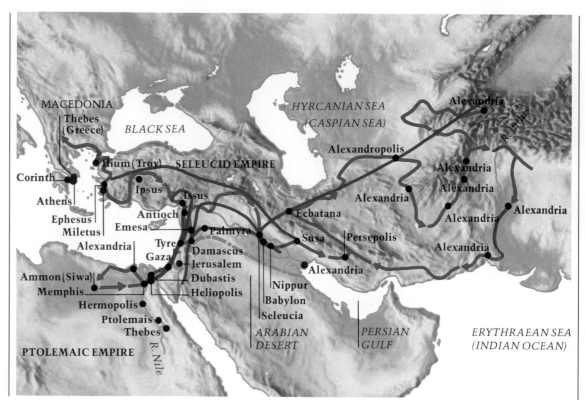

Seleucid and
Ptolemaic
Empires frontiers
in 2nd century BC

Alexander's route

Major trade
routes

MACEDONIA
Thebes
(Greece)
BLACK SEA
*HYRCANIAN SEA
(CASPIAN SEA)*
Alexandria
Ilium (Troy)   SELEUCID EMPIRE
Corinth
Alexandropolis
Ipsus
Athens   Issus   Alexandria   Alexandria
Antioch   Ecbatana   Alexandria
Ephesus   Emesa   Palmyra
Miletus   Susa   Persepolis
Alexandria   Tyre   Damascus
Gaza   Jerusalem   Alexandria
Ammon (Siwa)   Dubastis   Alexandria
Memphis   Heliopolis   Nippur
Hermopolis   Babylon
Ptolemais   Seleucia
Thebes   *ARABIAN
DESERT*   *PERSIAN
GULF*   *ERYTHRAEAN SEA
(INDIAN OCEAN)*
R. Nile
PTOLEMAIC EMPIRE

potamia and destroyed the Persian royal palaces at Persepolis. With a new army recruited in Persia, Alexander pressed on to Ecbatana and eastwards as far as the upper reaches of the River Indus. On his return to Babylon, Alexander declared that he had united east and west under his divine rule and began to build a fleet with which to conquer the world.

A fever cut short his plans, and Alexander died in Babylon at the age of 33. He had managed to impose a single rule on a larger part of the western world than anyone before him, but his empire did not survive his death when his generals divided it between themselves and then fought each other.

= Palestine and the Ptolemies =

Egypt was obtained by the general Ptolemy, and remained under the rule of the Ptolemies until the Romans conquered it in 30 BC. Under their rule, Alexandria rose in importance to become the greatest trading centre in the ancient world and a major centre of learn-

ABOVE *Alexander the Great's military genius ensured the overthrow of the Persian empire. Alexander proceeded to subdue the whole of the Near and Middle East, founding cities everywhere which were named after him. He died on his way back from India in Babylon in 321 BC. His conquests were later divided into the Seleucid and Ptolemaic empires centred in Asia Minor and Egypt respectively.*

ing. It also developed into a multi-racial community where foreign groups could live by their own customs and laws within the city's constitution, and consequently a large Jewish community settled there and thrived.

Immediately after Alexander's death, Palestine was ruled by the Seleucids, the dynasty founded by Alexander's companion, Seleucus. However, Palestine once more became a battle ground between two contesting powers and it was effectively ruled by the Ptolemies of Egypt until the end of the third century BC. Like everywhere else in the areas Alexander had conquered, Palestine and the Jews came under influence of Greek culture. Although Aramaic continued as the language of the country districts and the poor, the educated classes turned to Greek as the cities established schools, theatres, Greek theatres and gymnasia. Alexander had settled his veteran soldiers in colonies in Palestine, as elsewhere, and these were also centres for Greek ways, for everywhere cities old and new were laid out on Greek lines, with Greek architecture and street plans which reflected the desire for clear, rational order.

By this time, the 'dispersed' Jews of the

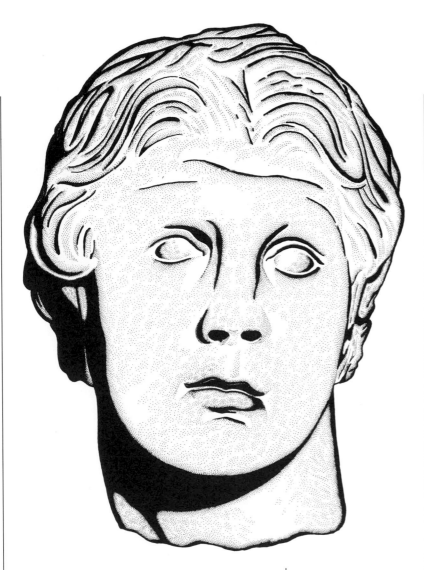

Greek ways of thinking to the traditional Hebrew beliefs about the world and man's relationship with God. The result is the collection of biblical material sometimes called the 'wisdom books', in which 'wisdom' is the practical knowledge of all that is necessary for stable government and a satisfying way of life.

Three of the 'wisdom' books of the Bible are collections of traditional Hebrew proverbs and sayings about correct conduct: Proverbs, Wisdom and Ecclesiasticus. There are also long passages which reflect characteristically Greek ideas, especially where wisdom is presented as the agent or assistant of God in the creation of the universe.

Another prominent theme in the 'wisdom' books is the beauty and grandeur of the natural world, as evidence for the creative power of God. The most explicitly Greek themes occur in such books as Job and Ecclesiastes, which demonstrate the limitations of human reason. The fundamental questions about suffering and the transitory nature of all human achievement are taken to their limits to show that there are no human answers except an agnosticism in the presence of the omniscience of God.

Diaspora far outnumbered Jews living in Palestine itself, and most Jews, whether in Palestine or elsewhere, no longer used Hebrew but Greek as their everyday language. Except for ceremonial purposes and in worship, Hebrew became a dead tongue, so to meet the needs of Jews who could no longer read Hebrew the Jewish sacred books were translated into Greek. This Greek version of the Old Testament is called the Septuagint, after the belief that it was produced by 70 scholars working separately, who agreed on ever word.

Greek Influence

The influence of Greek ways of thought can be seen in many ways in the books of the Old Testament, and in other Hebrew books written or edited in the centuries following Alexander the Great. Hebrew authors applied

ABOVE *Alexander the Great (356–323 BC) did perhaps more than any other individual to spread Greek influence and ideals. He was both a brilliant individual and a brilliant general, and his military successes no doubt owed something to his ability to understand and accept to some extent the ideas and ways of life of the peoples his armies mastered.*

For a century or more after the death of Alexander the Great, the Jews of Palestine lived under the rule of the Greek Ptolemies, who controlled Egypt. It was a comfortable relationship, as Palestine was the immediate neighbour of Egypt and large numbers of Jews were settled in Egyptian cities, particularly Alexandria.

All that changed in 198 BC when an upheaval typical of the ancient Near East moved Palestine from the control of the Ptolemies to the Seleucid rulers of Mesopotamia. It was an exchange of one Greek ruler for another, but it broke the bond between the influential Jews of Jerusalem and their Egyptian rulers.

Civil War

At first, the Seleucid kings allowed the Palestinian Jews to continue their traditional way of life without hindrance, but then they increased taxation and began to interfere with Jewish beliefs and practices. Among the Jews of Jerusalem and Judah there was a wide mixture of attitudes towards the Jewish religion. At one extreme were Jews who embraced the Greek way of life enthusiastically, with support for the theatre and the gymnasium; at the other extreme were Jews who maintained the strictest and narrowest interpretations of Hebrew law. A bloody civil war broke out with Jews crucifying each other over their interpretations of Judaism. The Seleucid emperor Antiochus chose to treat it all as rebellion and plundered the Temple in Jerusalem.

Antiochus stopped all the religious privileges enjoyed by the Jews, such as observation of the Sabbath and the traditional festivals. He forebade Jews to circumcise their sons and ordered all the Hebrew sacred books to be destroyed. An altar of the Greek god Zeus was erected in the Temple and pigs were sacrificed on it. Jews throughout Palestine were forced to take part in what they regarded as idolatrous and pagan worship.

Independence

The action of the Seleucid emperor provoked an organized rebellion of Jews led by Judas Maccabeus, which eventually ended in the defeat of the Greeks and Jewish independence in Palestine. At the time, Antiochus was also fighting the Parthians in the eastern part of his empire, so the guerrilla forces of the Maccabees were able to win a series of victories against Greek armies. Despite setbacks, Judas was able to take Jerusalem from the Greeks in 164 BC, clear the Temple of all traces of non-Jewish worship and rededicate it to the Hebrew God, Yahweh. The ceremony is still commemorated in an important Jewish religious festival, the Feast of Dedication.

Judas Maccabeus defeated and killed the Greek general Nicanor in 160 BC, but later in the same year Judas himself was killed. His brother Jonathan took over the leadership and held it from 160 to 143 BC. However, he

RIGHT *The Greek theatre at Samaria north of Jerusalem. The city of Samaria gave its* *name to the Samaritans, so greatly detested by the Jews in New Testament times.*

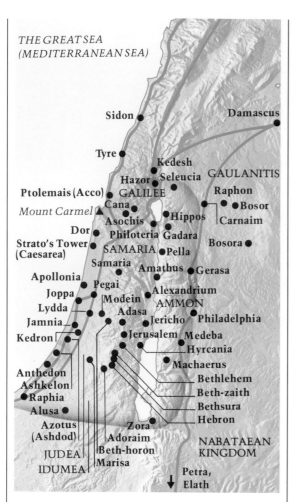

THE GREAT SEA
(MEDITERRANEAN SEA)

Sidon

Damascus

Tyre

Kedesh
Hazor · Seleucia   GAULANITIS
Ptolemais (Acco) · GALILEE   Raphon
Mount Carmel · Cana   Bosor
Asochis · Hippos   Carnaim
Dor · Philoteria · Gadara
Strato's Tower · SAMARIA · Pella   Bosora
(Caesarea)
Samaria
Apollonia   Amathus · Gerasa
Joppa · Pegai
Lydda · Modein   Alexandrium
Jamnia · Adasa   AMMON
Kedron · Jericho   Philadelphia
Jerusalem · Medeba
Hyrcania
Machaerus
Anthedon   Bethlehem
Ashkelon   Beth-zaith
Raphia   Bethsura
Alusa   Hebron
Azotus   Zora
(Ashdod)   Adoraim   NABATAEAN
JUDEA   Beth-horon   KINGDOM
IDUMEA   Marisa
Petra,
Elath

was imprisoned and murdered and another Maccabee brother, Simon, stepped into the leadership. The Jews of Palestine could at least hope that they were in control of their own lives.

Jewish Strife

It would be a relief to report that the victories of the Maccabees ushered in a period of peace and tranquility for the Jews of Jerusalem during the first century BC, but this was far from the case. The different factions within the Jewish state, centred on Jerusalem, fought each other bitterly for power. Although the Jews managed to extend their rule to the very borders of the old Davidic empire, internal tensions reached such a state of civil war that both sides appealed to the Romans to come

and restore order.

The Roman general Pompey entered Jerusalem in 63 BC, captured the Temple (which was being defended by the current Jewish king and high priest), and made Palestine part of the Roman province of Syria. The latest brief period of Jewish independence had not even lasted a hundred years, and it was to be the last one until AD 1948.

Jews Abroad

The Old Testament cannot be understood without appreciating the importance of the international routes which ran through Palestine and connected it with the major centres of civilization in the ancient world. It would have been surprising if the Jews of Palestine—the Holy Land—had not taken

RIGHT *Reflections on water, the giver of life and a particularly precious commodity in the arid and semi-arid regions of the Near and Middle East. The Greek appreciation of the beauty of nature influenced some of the most beautiful passages of the Old Testament.*

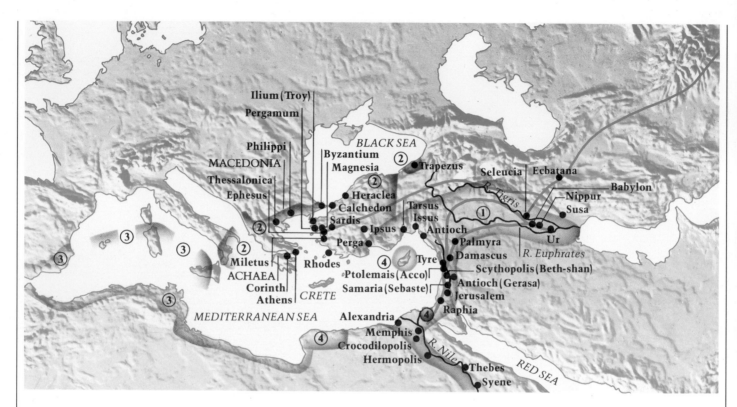

ILIUM (Troy)
Pergamum
Philippi
MACEDONIA
Thessalonica
Ephesus
Byzantium
Magnesia
BLACK SEA
②
Trapezus
②
②
Seleucia
Ecbatana
Babylon
Nippur
Susa
Heraclea
Calchedon
Sardis
Ipsus
Perga
Tarsus
Issus
Antioch
①
R. Tigris
Ur
R. Euphrates
②
②
Miletus
ACHAEA
Corinth
Athens
Rhodes
CRETE
④
Ptolemais (Acco)
Samaria (Sebaste)
Tyre
Palmyra
Damascus
Scythopolis (Beth-shan)
Antioch (Gerasa)
Jerusalem
Raphia
③
③
③
③
MEDITERRANEAN SEA
Alexandria
④
Memphis
Crocodilopolis
Hermopolis
④
R. Nile
Thebes
Syene
RED SEA

advantage of these routes to establish Jewish settlements in all of the trading centres of the Near and Middle East. In fact, there are references to groups of Hebrew settlements outside Palestine long before the great deportations began with the Assyrian destruction of the northern Hebrew kingdom of Israel in 721 BC and the Babylonian deportation of Judean Hebrews in 598 and 587 BC.

Many Jews had fled to Egypt to escape the Babylonians, and there are records of Jewish mercenaries serving Egypt as frontier guards in Cyrenaica, Libya and the regions east of the Nile delta. When the empires of the Greeks and of Rome opened administrative and communication links between the Near East and the rest of the Mediterranean area, there was a marked increase in the numbers of Jews living outside Palestine; both Rome and Alexandria had large Jewish colonies.

The Synagogue

Although the Jews beyond Palestine recognized that Jerusalem and its Temple was

ABOVE *Alexandria, on the Mediterranean coast north of Memphis, was the greatest city built by Alexander and was later the largest city and main cultural centre of the Mediterranean. One of its most important treasures was a Greek translation of the Old Testament made there by Jewish scholars – the Jewish community in Alexandria was the most numerous Jewish expatriate population of the time.*

— *Major trade routes*
① *Jewish settlement areas before 500 BC*
② *Jewish settlement extension after Alexander*
Movement of the Diaspora:
③ *Jews of Carthage*
④ *Settlements of Jews established under Egyptian supervision*

their spiritual home where they must journey to take part in Jewish sacrificial worship, and which they generously supported through special taxes, they also made provision for corporate Jewish worship in their home towns and cities. Wherever Jews lived they founded synagogues as the distinctive Jewish meeting places for prayers, reverence of the sacred books, sacred readings, discussion, and instruction of the young. Synagogues also spread in Palestine itself as the regulations restricting sacrifice to the Temple in Jerusalem were enforced; it was more difficult to get to Jerusalem from northern Palestine than it was from Alexandria in Egypt.

More and more, the Jews became people of the book—the Old Testament—translated into their native languages, whether Greek, Syriac, Aramaic or, increasingly, Latin. Hebrew always remained important as the sacred language of worship and law, but the Jewish religion never became an esoteric faith only to be embraced by an elite who could understand a dead language. Jerusalem became the great centre of pilgrimage, but the local synagogue was the place where the faith was learned, practised and preserved.

RIGHT *The Jewish kings appointed by the Romans built great fortresses such as this one at Masada. Herod the Great constructed many of the main fortifications between 37 and 31 BC. Masada later became a symbol of Jewish resistance to foreign rule.*

LEFT *The synagogue at Capernaum. Capernaum is on the northern shore of the Sea of Galilee where Jesus once stayed. Although this synagogue was built a little after the time of the Bible, these magnificent ruins at Capernaum make it clear how important the synagogue had already become to local Jewish settlements.*

CHAPTER 5

Christianity

The Romans

By the time Jesus Christ was born, the whole of the Mediterranean area was under the firm control of Rome. Palestine was once more both a frontier region and a vital link in the communications between a great power and outlying provinces of its empire. Neither Jesus nor any other Jew could escape the influence of Rome.

The secret of Rome's conquest of the rest of the Mediterranean world lay in the way her citizens approached military service. In the earlier part of her expansion every citizen of Rome was conscripted into the army in rotation. They willingly accepted the very different kind of discipline necessary for effective military service, and were led into battle by the magistrates they themselves had elected to office. The army was thus a civilian 'militia' in which there were clear and consistent procedures for all military situations, from the pitching of camp to the assault of a fortified stronghold.

Every citizen was trained in these military procedures so that a conscript during his period of duty, or the magistrates in office for that year, could take over without confusion. All that was needed to make such a force effective was mobility, and this the Roman state ensured from 312 BC when it built the first of the great military roads, the Via Appia. These would eventually form a vast network of communication lines linking every part of the Roman empire.

Religion and Family

Roman religion emphasized the sacredness of the family and the home by revering the spirits of the family's ancestors, and by worship of the household gods at the domestic altar in each home. The father was the family's priest, whose authority within the family—and as its representative in the city's assemblies—was absolute.

This same sense of the sacred was felt towards the natural world, and led to the characteristic Roman practice of looking for omens in natural phenomena, or in the entrails of sacrificed animals, to discover whether the gods favoured whatever was

RIGHT *The Forum in Rome at dawn. From its origins as a small city on the River Tiber, Rome grew and developed as the administrative centre for the whole of the Mediterranean region from Egypt to Britain.*

about to be undertaken. The chief gods of the Roman state were Jupiter and Mars. Jupiter was the supreme deity and god of the heavens. Mars was god of war; he also controlled the growth of the crops and the harvest during the season of the year when warfare was most practicable and the citizen army was torn between farm and camp.

Expansion

At the time when the Jews were struggling to rebuild Jerusalem after the Babylonian exile —500 BC—Rome was still no more than a small city on the Palatine Hill, farming the surrounding country only as far as it could easily defend it. Gradually, the city extended its control over its neighbours, first by enter-

ABOVE *The outline of a Roman camp on the shores of the Dead Sea. The design of Roman camps would have varied little throughout the Roman empire.*

ing into league with them, then by leading them in times of danger, and finally by conquering them, until Rome ruled all central Italy.

The first real conflict between Rome and people beyond Italy came when the Greek colony of Tarentum hired King Pyrrhus of Epirus to defend them against the Romans. Pyrrhus defeated the Romans, but he incurred such heavy losses (the 'pyrrhic victory') that he eventually deserted the Greeks who had hired him, leaving them no choice but to accept an alliance with Rome.

Carthage and Africa

Until the Romans defeated it, the dominant power in the western Mediterranean was

Carthage (modern Tunis) which was a strong sea power. The long series of wars between Carthage and Rome lasted from 264 to 146 BC, with periods of truce and times when Rome thought it had beaten Carthage into complete submission. During the early stages of the conflict the Romans were forced to fight at sea, and had to build a fleet and learn naval tactics.

In the second of the wars with Carthage, which began in 218 BC, the Carthaginian general Hannibal took the conflict to Italy and attacked Rome from the north with the aid of the famous elephants which his army had led across the Alps. By the time of the third war in 146 BC Rome had become a great military power, and the conflict ended swiftly with the destruction of Carthage. The city was ploughed, and the fields were sown with salt and its citizens were sold into slavery.

ABOVE *Natural water courses and artificial ones. The aqueducts that still survive in different parts of the empire, such as the one at Neapolis in Macedonia which carried water for irrigation in Paul's time, are a fine tribute to the skills of the Roman architects and engineers. Most aqueducts were built to carry water from natural springs to cities, often over distances of many miles.*

Spain and Palestine

By 205 BC Rome had made itself master of Spain at the western end of the Mediterranean, and by 147 BC it had extended its power eastwards into Greece and Macedonia. By now the city was sole ruler of most of the Mediterranean and its possessions were bringing enormous wealth and power to its citizens. Asia Minor first felt the might of a Roman army in 133 BC, but for the moment Roman expansion was halted by civil war in Rome itself as rival generals, including Julius Caesar, manoeuvered for power. The dissentions which tore Rome apart were only

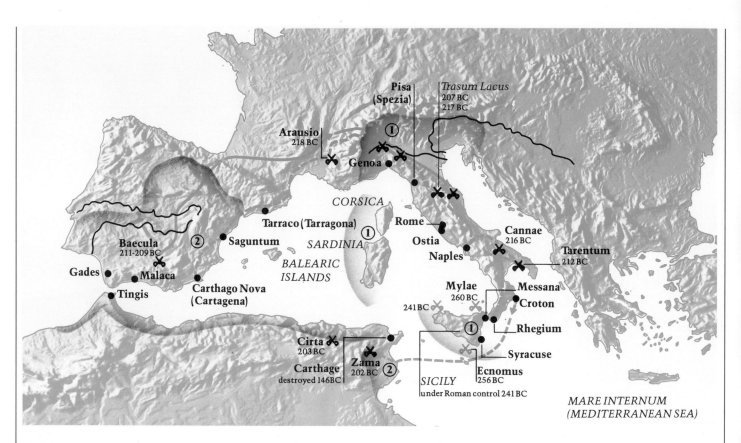

Pisa
(Spezia)

Trasum Lacus
207 BC
217 BC

Arausio
218 BC

Genoa

①

CORSICA

Rome

Cannae
216 BC

Tarraco (Tarragona)

①

Ostia

Tarentum
212 BC

Baecula
211-209 BC

②

Saguntum

SARDINIA

Naples

*BALEARIC
ISLANDS*

Mylae
260 BC

Messana

Gades

Croton

Malaca

241 BC

Tingis

Carthago Nova
(Cartagena)

①

Rhegium

Cirta
203 BC

Syracuse

Zama
202 BC

②

Ecnomus
256 BC

Carthage
destroyed 146 BC

SICILY
under Roman control 241 BC

*MARE INTERNUM
(MEDITERRANEAN SEA)*

stopped when the citizens voted power to a single person who would wield absolute authority as emperor and dictator.

The Jews of Judah and Jerusalem were also deep in civil war after 90 years of freedom from Greek rule. Both sides in the Jewish conflict appealed to Rome to restore order under an old treaty of mutual aid. The Romans entered Jerusalem in 63 BC and immediately earned the enmity of conservative Jews by entering the forbidden inner sanctuary of the Temple.

In 30 BC Rome completed its conquest of the whole Mediterranean coast by taking Egypt, thus bringing to an end the rule of the Ptolemies.

The Religions of the Empire

The bewildering array of faiths and gods worshipped in the Roman empire reflected the many different needs felt by people in an age when famine, disease and war were normal experiences. The Bible asserts fiercely

ABOVE *Rome and Carthage vied with each other for political and economic control of the western Mediterranean. The third Roman campaign ended in 146 BC with Carthage razed to the ground.*

① *Territory of Rome*

② *Territory of Carthage*

✗ *Roman naval victories in the First Punic Wars (264–241 BC)*

✗ *Battle sites during the Second Punic Wars (218–201 BC)*

— *Hasdrubal (209–207 BC)*

--- *Hannibal (219–202 BC)*

that Jews were totally loyal to a single religious tradition handed down to them unchanged from Moses, but it is clear also that they were deeply influenced by other religious traditions and borrowed freely from them.

In the deeply corrupt and insecure ancient world there was a real need for salvation, and many religions provided saviour-gods. Some were heroes who were born of unions between gods and humans; others were manifestations of gods who disguised themselves temporarily as humans in order to intervene in human affairs. In many minds, this accounted for the successes of an Alexander or an Augustus Caesar, and worship of such great rulers reinforced the authority of the state and its stability.

Sometimes the sacredness of the gods was heightened by secrecy and by rites which expressed the worshippers' sense of awe. Some stories about the gods showed them how the gods met human needs, such as the fertility pattern of the agricultural year. These 'mystery' religions were practised throughout the Roman empire with vivid

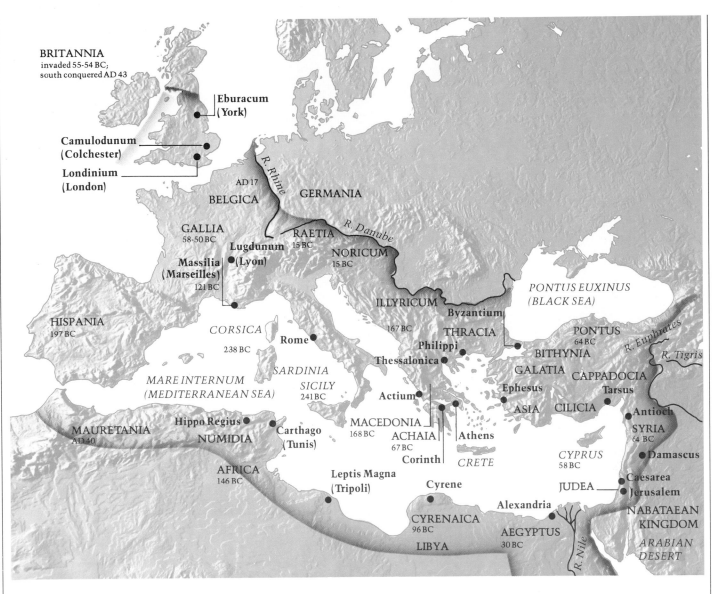

Eburacum
(York)

Camulodunum
(Colchester)

Londinium
(London)

AD 17

BELGICA

GERMANIA

R. Rhine

GALLIA
58-50 BC

RAETIA
15 BC

R. Danube

Lugdunum
(Lyon)

NORICUM
15 BC

Massilia
(Marseilles)
121 BC

ILLYRICUM
167 BC

PONTUS EUXINUS
(BLACK SEA)

Byzantium

HISPANIA
197 BC

CORSICA

238 BC

Rome

THRACIA

Philippi

PONTUS
64 BC

R. Euphrates

R. Tigris

BITHYNIA

Thessalonica

GALATIA

CAPPADOCIA

MARE INTERNUM
(MEDITERRANEAN SEA)

SARDINIA

SICILY
241 BC

Actium

Ephesus

Tarsus

ASIA

CILICIA

Antioch

MAURETANIA
AD 40

Hippo Regius

NUMIDIA

Carthago
(Tunis)

MACEDONIA
168 BC

ACHAIA
67 BC

Athens

Corinth

CRETE

CYPRUS
58 BC

SYRIA
64 BC

Damascus

AFRICA
146 BC

Leptis Magna
(Tripoli)

Cyrene

Alexandria

JUDEA

Caesarea

Jerusalem

NABATAEAN
KINGDOM

CYRENAICA
96 BC

AEGYPTUS
30 BC

LIBYA

R. Nile

ARABIAN
DESERT

rites of initiation which admitted members to salvation. In some 'mysteries' worshippers were drenched in the blood of sacrificial bulls as a symbol of sharing in the life and powers of the creator gods.

The powers of nature and the 'heavenly' bodies—the sun, moon, planets and stars— were worshipped in animal or human form, and everywhere astrology was taken seriously as a guide to right action. As most people were illiterate, religious faith was expressed visually, through ritual, dance, drama, temple architecture and representations of the gods and goddesses. Small statues of gods and goddesses have been unearthed in enormous

ABOVE *The Roman empire at its height stretched from Britain, Spain and Mauretania in the West across central Europe, Turkey and North Africa to the eastern end of the Mediterranean.*

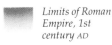 *Limits of Roman Empire, 1st century* AD

quantities from excavations of domestic sites in the Near East, showing that miniatures of the great temple statues were worshipped in most homes. The manufacture of images of Diana was such an important industry at Ephesus that the silversmiths accused Paul of endangering their trade by his preaching about Jesus.

As traders, officials and soldiers passed along the strategic routes through Palestine, the Jews were exposed to all the cultural and religious influences of the Roman empire. Galilee, where Jesus grew to manhood, was a crossing point for some of the busiest roads in the ancient world.

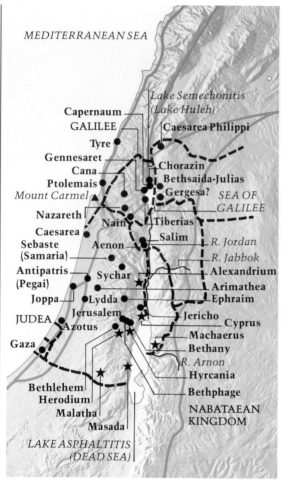

MEDITERRANEAN SEA

Lake Semechonitis
(Lake Huleh)

Capernaum
GALILEE
Caesarea Philippi
Tyre
Gennesaret
Cana
Chorazin
Ptolemais
Bethsaida-Julias
Mount Carmel
Gergesa?
SEA OF
GALILEE

Nazareth
Nain
Tiberias
Caesarea
Salim
Sebaste
Aenon
R. Jordan
(Samaria)
R. Jabbok
Antipatris
Alexandrium
(Pegai)
Sychar
Arimathea
Joppa
Lydda
Ephraim
JUDEA
Jerusalem
Jericho
Azotus
Cyprus
Machaerus
Gaza
Bethany
R. Arnon
Hyrcania
Bethphage
Bethlehem
NABATAEAN
Herodium
KINGDOM
Malatha
Masada
LAKE ASPHALTITIS
(DEAD SEA)

The Jews

By the time Palestine was incorporated into the Roman empire during the first century BC, Jews already enjoyed special status and privileges which were to last until the Roman-Jewish war of AD 66–70, and even then the payment of a special tax gave them freedom to practise their exclusive religion. Jews living outside Palestine had long out-numbered the Palestinian Jews, and by New Testament times in the first century AD there were Jewish communities throughout the empire.

The local synagogue was the centre of community life and worship for the Jews of the 'dispersion' or 'diaspora', as it was too for most Jews in Palestine who could not easily reach the Temple in Jerusalem. The Acts of the Apostles shows that there was a synagogue in every town with a Jewish community. Jerusalem remained the true focus for every Jew's religion and loyalty, for Jerusalem contained the Temple, the only place on earth where the full rites of the Jewish religion could be celebrated.

ABOVE LEFT *The amphitheatre in Amman, the capital of Jordan, is one of the most impressive monuments to the Roman conquest.*

ABOVE RIGHT *The ruins of some of the fortresses built in Palestine by Herod the Great can still be seen. The fortresses were all destroyed by the Romans in AD 73.*

★   *Fortresses*

- - -   *Political boundaries*

   Major trade routes

Herod's Temple

In 22 BC the Jewish puppet king, Herod the Great (37–4 BC) began to rebuild the Temple of Jerusalem on a magnificent scale as a gift to his long-suffering people. The work continued for 80 years without interruption of worship, but six years after it was finally completed the new Temple was destroyed at the climax of the Jewish war with Rome in AD 70. Its site is now occupied by the magnificent Dome of the Rock, the Muslim shrine build in AD 691, and there only remain the great stones of the platform on which Herod's Temple stood.

The complex daily round of worship and all the activities associated with the Temple were administered by a hierarchy of priests of various grades and families, who maintained the structure and controlled its use.

The High Priest, appointed by the Roman administration, presided over the supreme Jewish court and was in effect the leader of Jews throughout the empire. Trumpet calls echoed through the city at the times of sacrifice, which ranged from the lambs sacrificed every morning and evening, to the hundreds of animals sacrificed at the Passover and the great pilgrimage festivals. Only priests could enter the Temple building itself, men were allowed into an innermost court, women in the next court, furthest from the Temple, and foreigners were forbidden from all but the outermost court, under pain of death.

The Scrolls of Qumran

The discovery in 1948 of ancient manuscripts hidden in caves at Qumran near the Dead Sea added greatly to modern knowledge about the Jewish religion in Palestine during the first centuries BC and AD. The vast collection of writings unearthed by archaeologists included whole books or sections of books from the whole of the Hebrew Bible.

In addition there were other religious writings very similar to parts of the Bible, and documents about the organization and life of a Jewish religious community.

Members of this communty believed that the real meaning of the sacred scriptures had been revealed by a 'Teacher of Righteousness' who had been the community's founder, and that the members of the community had been chosen to be 'Sons of Light' in the conflict with the 'Sons of Darkness'. God would finally send a prophet and two messiahs to bring the conflict to a victorious conclusion and to dispense justice.

Jesus and his Followers

All the information we have about Jesus comes from the people who knew him during his lifetime, from his birth about 5 BC (before Herod the Great died in 4 BC), to his crucifixion and—Christians believe—his resurrection in AD 30. As Jesus himself left nothing in writing, all the information in the four Gospels of the New Testament has its origins

LEFT *Excavations around the Temple area in Jerusalem have shown that it was the centre of a vast complex of buildings housing the Jewish authorities' administrative headquarters at the time of the Romans.*

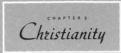

ABOVE *Nazareth, 15 miles (24 km) west of the Sea of Galilee, was an insignificant provincial town when Jesus's parents took him to live there. It is now a major pilgrimage attraction.*

in the family of Jesus and in the followers whom he chose to be close to him. Naturally, the information is coloured by their beliefs and experiences.

After the death of Jesus, his disciples were convinced that he had risen from the dead, and that they had been given a share in his risen life and in his freedom from death as the Son of God. Consequently they looked on the death and resurrection of Jesus as the new covenant with God, and on themselves

as the new chosen people through whom God was offering salvation to the whole world.

Like Jesus himself, they were all Jews, and they continued at first to worship in the Temple of Jerusalem and in the Jewish synagogues, but they put a new interpretation on the Jewish Passover—the 'eucharist' or 'thanksgiving'—based on the actions and words of Jesus at the Passover meal he ate with his disciples just before his arrest and death.

89

The Teaching about Jesus

The Acts of the Apostles contains detailed reports of the sermons preached by Jesus's disciples in the years immediately following his death, and the teaching they gave is also reflected in the letters of the New Testament, most of which were written before the four Gospels as we now have them. The early sermons and the letters therefore give us an idea of the beliefs about Jesus which were to be the basis of the Gospels.

In their sermons, the disciples (by now 'apostles', ie people with authority) proclaimed that God's revelations of himself during the Old Testament period had reached their climax and fulfilment in the life, death and resurrection of Jesus. He was the 'Messiah', the 'Christ' (Hebrew and Greek, respectively, for the same title) who had come from God and had now returned to him, his work on earth completed, to be Lord of Creation as both man and God.

The Holy Spirit, they continued, had been sent to them to prove that Jesus now shared his powers with the members of the Christian community. The membership was open to all who turned to God, accepted Jesus as Lord, and received baptism. Their preaching ended with the promise that God would soon complete the whole plan of salvation with the second coming of Jesus and the general judgement of all people.

Support

The apostles supported their preaching and teaching with recollections of Jesus's life as they had witnessed it. They told of the things he did and said, and the people whom he met in the years leading up to his crucifixion and resurrection. They concentrated particularly on his last few days in Jerusalem at the Passover of AD 30.

As the disciples with personal knowledge of Jesus began to die or be executed, the Gospels were written to give a permanent and dependable record of what those disciples taught about Jesus, while there were still people alive who could vouch for their accuracy.

The first of the Gospels was written (in the form in which we now have them) about 30

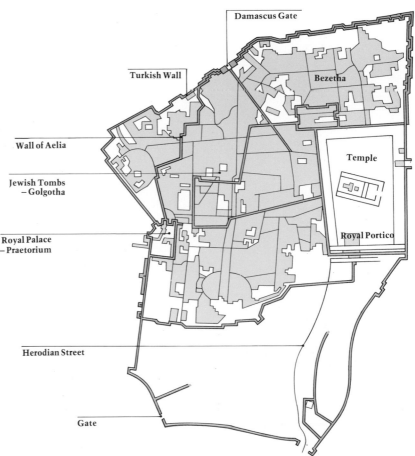

Damascus Gate

Turkish Wall

Bezetha

Wall of Aelia

Temple

Jewish Tombs
– Golgotha

Royal Palace
– Praetorium

Royal Portico

Herodian Street

Gate

ABOVE *Modern tourists in Jerusalem may mistakenly assume that they are seeing the Jerusalem of the New Testament, but it has been destroyed and rebuilt at least twice since then. Golgotha, or Calvary, the site of Jesus's crucifixion then lay well outside the city walls. The old parts of Jerusalem today are largely medieval.*

LEFT *Jesus's body was taken down from the cross and laid in an empty rock tomb similar to this one. The rolled back circular stone door was the first sign of Jesus's resurrection from the dead.*

years after the death of Jesus, and the other three appeared during the next 30 years. The rest of the New Testament ranges in date from about 15 years after the death of Jesus to the end of the first century AD.

Matthew's Gospel

Although it was not the first of the Gospels to be written in the form in which we now have them (that distinction belongs to Mark), Matthew's Gospel is the one which brings out most clearly the links between Jesus and the Old Testament religion of the Jews. Indeed, it opens with a detailed genealogy of Jesus's descent from Abraham, to whom God gave the first covenant making the Hebrews his chosen people, and it highlights King David as one of Jesus's most important ancestors. David again receives prominence when Matthew quotes the prophet Micah's

Major trade routes

★ Fortresses

RIGHT *The Sea of Galilee, even 2,000 years later, is still a place where one can be aware of the spirit of Jesus's early ministry.*

MEDITERRANEAN SEA

PROVINCE OF SYRIA

● Caesarea Philippi

Capernaum
Gennesaret
Ptolemais (Acco) ●
SEA OF GALILEE
Mount Carmel ▲
THE GREAT PLAIN
Dor ●
Caesarea ●
Roman headquarters

Bethsaida-Julias
GALILEE ● **Gergesa?**
● **Cana** **Hippos**
● **Nazareth** ● **Gadara**
Tiberias

TETRARCHY OF PHILIP

● **Scythopolis**
JUDEA ● **Pella**

DECAPOLIS

● **Sebaste (Samaria)**
● **Gerasa**

R. Jabbok

Alexandrium ★
Cyprus
Joppa ●
Ephraim ●
Emmaus ● **Jericho** ●
Jerusalem ●
Ashkelon ● **Bethlehem** ●
Bethany
Gaza ● **Herodium**
Hebron ●
Hyrcania

R. Jordan

Philadelphia

PEREA

● **Medeba**
Khirbet Qumran
'Dead Sea Scrolls'
★ **Machaerus**

R. Arnon

Masada ★

IDUMEA

★
Malatha

NABATAEAN KINGDOM

LAKE ASPHALTITIS (DEAD SEA)

ABOVE *Caesarea, on the Mediterranean coast, was an important commercial port and the military centre of the Roman administration. Jerusalem was garrisoned but was only a secondary base. There was* also a council of 71 Jews, over which the high priest presided, however the council's authority was limited. After the Jewish–Roman war of AD 70, the Roman Emperor Vespasian asserted personal control over Judea, southern Palestine, letting it out to tenant farmers, after the Jewish–Roman war of AD 66– 70. The settlement of Khirbet Qumran and the 'Dead Sea Scrolls' also date from this period.

prophecy about Bethlehem, King David's birthplace and the place where Jesus was born. The message is clear: Jesus is the new Abraham, the new Moses and the new David, sent by God to give his people a new covenant and to be their lawgiver and king as he leads them through death into the freedom of eternal life.

The whole of Matthew's Gospel breathes the atmosphere of Jewish rabbinical thought, with which the first Jewish Christians would have been so familiar from the readings and discussions in the synagogues. This is most noticeable in the five collections of the sayings of Jesus which are such a feature of Matthew, especially the most famous of them, the

ABOVE *The Jordan, the longest and most important river in Palestine. For the followers of Jesus, his baptism in the River Jordan marked the beginning of his reign as messianic king, and a Jewish cleansing rite became the way to citizenship of the Kingdom of God.*

Sermon on the Mount. This is where Jesus takes a section of the Law of Moses and comments on them in the light of his special understanding of their significance as the law of the new covenant. Seen in this light, Matthew is a guide for Christian conduct written to meet the needs of Jewish Christians as they turned from their old religion or were expelled from the synagogues.

But the whole Gospel moves steadily towards its climax with Jesus's last few days, for the emphasis is not so much on the teaching Jesus gave as on his actions, particularly the miracles he performed. These all point forward to the cross and the empty tomb, to ensure that Christianity could not be treated as just another philosophy or 'mystery' religion. Nor does Matthew support the beliefs of some of the first Christians who taught that you had to become a Jew to be a good Christian. There are strong denunciations of such Jewish groups as the Pharisees and Sadducees, who emphasized the exclusive privileges (and responsibilities) of the Jews as the chosen people of God.

Mark's Gospel

The New Testament adapts the central message of Christianity to the needs of people with different cultural backgrounds, and this is particularly noticeable in the case of the four Gospels. The main difference was between Christians with Jewish backgrounds and those brought up in Hellenistic (Greek) ways of thought and behaviour. Rome itself was deeply influenced by Greek culture, and many scholars think that Mark's Gospel was written with the Christians of Rome in mind.

If this is the case, it would appeal to people who are impressed by the way the character and abilities of a person are revealed in their actions, for unlike Matthew, there is much less emphasis in Mark on the Jewish inheritance of Jesus. The pattern of action is particularly well expressed in the way Mark selects a special sequence of miracles to demonstrate the special nature of Jesus's powers and the way he used them.

The miracles show Jesus with the kind of powers over the natural world which only a creator-god could have, who then uses these powers to overcome any evil which tries to oppose him and to heal people of the defects and imperfections which hinder them from reaching the perfection God intends for them. Mark emphasizes that Jesus will not use any of his powers—even that he cannot use them—without human co-operation. People must have faith in him if he is to help them, and he fails in his own home town of Nazareth when the people who knew him so well could not believe that he really was the Son of God.

All this is carefully structured to point forward to the accounts in Mark of the Last Supper, the crucifixion and the brief record of the resurrection. Seen against the background of the miracles Jesus had performed,

ABOVE *The Via Dolorosa in Jerusalem marks the traditional route taken by Jesus from Pilate's court to Golgotha, which in Hebrew means skull, the place outside the walls of Jerusalem where criminals were executed. Excavations reveal that the soldiers' guardroom was near this spot.*

his sufferings become the patience of love in the face of evil, and his resurrection the overcoming of all human imperfections, even death itself, in order to be united with God.

This Gospel would have had special appeal for the Christians of Rome if experiencing the first sharp persecutions of Christians as Nero shifted the blame onto them for the great fire of Rome in AD 64.

Luke's Gospel and Acts

The New Testament contains not only a Gospel written by Luke, but also the sequel

Luke wrote, which is longer than the Gospel, and develops the same themes over the 30 years following the death of Jesus. These two books, the Gospel and the Acts of the Apostles, were written for the non-Jewish Christians of Asia Minor and Greece, reached by Paul on his three missonary journeys.

Luke was a close companion of Paul, mentioned in three of his letters, and it is clear from Acts that Luke accompanied Paul on some of his journeys. There are four places where the narrative changes from the 'he' or 'they' form to 'we', which suggests that Luke was with Paul in those places.

Understandably, then, Luke's Gospel and Acts emphasize that Jesus is the saviour sent by God to save all mankind, no matter what their race or class. Even if God did work through the Jews as his chosen instruments until the coming of Jesus, Luke brings out incidents to show that they have now rejected him and a new era has begun. If anything, outcasts and the disadvantaged sections of the Roman world are sought out by Jesus for special consideration. Women are treated as the equals of men, and all people are freely and equally pardoned by Jesus when they turn to him. The poor shepherds of Bethlehem are summoned by angels to be the first to know about the newly-born Jesus and to worship him.

Luke presents Jesus as the agent of God's omnipotence, the climax of all previous history and the beginning of the new era of salvation which will reach the whole world. This message is even conveyed by the literary structure of Luke's two volumes, which are organized as series of journeys. The Gospel starts in the obscurity of Nazareth and then presents all the information about Jesus as a series of journeys to Jerusalem, the centre of the Jewish religion, which Jesus replaces in his own person. Acts takes the journey theme from Jerusalem in ever wider sweeps among the non-Jews of the Roman world until it reaches Rome itself, the centre of the new era. Christianity, claims Luke, is the religion of the new world order with Jesus as the real ruler of it.

Everywhere in Luke's writings there are references to the Holy Spirit: at the conception and birth of Jesus, his baptism at the start of his ministry, and in Jesus's own explanation of his powers to the citizens of Nazareth. In Acts the Holy Spirit is the explanation for the

ABOVE *The Pool of Bethesda, the cistern where the sacrificial animals for the Temple were washed was also the scene of one of Jesus's miracles, for which the authorities were all the more anxious to kill him.*

LEFT *The Mary Magdalene Church. From the Mount of Olives the site of the Temple is visible past the domes of the Church of St Mary Magdalene. Mary Magdalene appears in the New Testament as a woman whose evil spirit was cast out by Jesus and she then acknowledged his saving power. Luke emphasizes the special honour accorded to women by Jesus.*

extraordinary success of the new religion as it reaches out from Jerusalem to Rome. Again, it is made clear that this force is available to each individual freely, and is the only effective means of realizing the Greek ideals of equality and justice.

John's Gospel

The last of the four Gospels presents Jesus in a very different light from the other three: it uses a different chronology, it only gives details of seven miracles, and it has a very different style.

To understand John it is necessary to appreciate something of the religions which appealed to many of the professional classes in the Roman empire, such as the career army officers. These were attracted by the 'mystery' religions which developed in Greece and Egypt after the old classical religion of the Greek gods ceased to meet the needs of educated people.

These religious movements opened the secrets of the universe to their members: the origins and destiny of man, the forces behind the cycle of the agricultural year, strength to withstand evil and suffering, and ways of prolonging life beyond death or of ensuring the safe passage of the soul. Secret knowledge

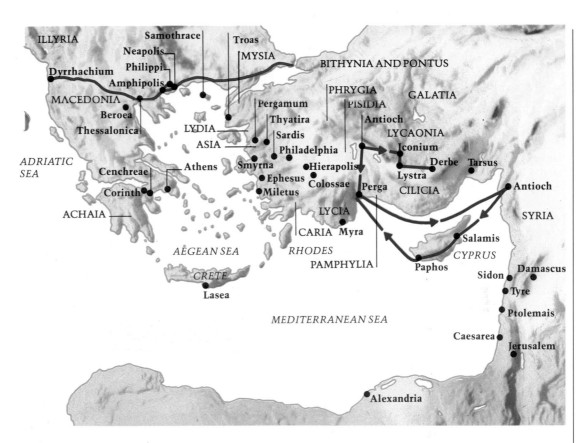

ILLYRIA
Samothrace
Troas
Neapolis
MYSIA
Philippi
Dyrrhachium
Amphipolis
BITHYNIA AND PONTUS
MACEDONIA
Pergamum
PHRYGIA
GALATIA
Beroea
Thyatira
PISIDIA
Thessalonica
LYDIA
Sardis
Antioch
ADRIATIC SEA
ASIA
Philadelphia
LYCAONIA
Iconium
Athens
Smyrna
Hierapolis
Derbe
Tarsus
Cenchreae
Ephesus
Colossae
Lystra
Antioch
Corinth
Miletus
Perga
CILICIA
SYRIA
ACHAIA
LYCIA
Damascus
AEGEAN SEA
CARIA
Myra
Sidon
RHODES
CYPRUS
Tyre
PAMPHYLIA
Salamis
CRETE
Paphos
Ptolemais
Lasea
Caesarea
MEDITERRANEAN SEA
Jerusalem

Alexandria

was conveyed through complex symbolic rites, and adherents were bound by the strictest oaths to keep the secrets revealed to them.

John presents Jesus as the real secret behind the forces of history and of nature, now revealed to all. He is the 'word' of creation, says John, a concept which combines the Greek idea of pattern or logic at the heart of the ever-changing world, with the Hebrew idea of the universe as the product of God's word of command where history unfolds as God speaks to his prophets.

This is then developed by John throughout the Gospel by symbolism which shows that everything done and said by Jesus has a deeper meaning. The wine Jesus produces from water at the wedding feast of Cana symbolizes blood and life and sacrifice. When he drives the traders from the Temple in Jerusalem it indicates that he is the new Temple which will be built anew in three days after his crucifixion. The healing of a blind man is explained at great length as the indication that Jesus is the light of the world. When he restores his friend Lazarus to life

ABOVE *It was largely as a result of Paul's missionary journeys that Christianity spread from Palestine throughout the Roman Empire.*

— *Paul's 1st missionary journey*

— *Egnatian Way*

Jesus explains that he himself is the resurrection and the life, and that whoever believes in him will live, even though he dies.

Presented in this way, the words and deeds of Jesus reveal him as the power which brought the universe into existence and which guides history. He is also a power of love prepared to agonize over the death of his friend, be moved by the sufferings of the sick and poor, and to go to the cross to save mankind. The secret of the universe has been revealed openly as love, says John, and everyone can share in it.

Galilee and Jerusalem

To the Roman world, Christianity was at first nothing more than a Jewish sect, just one of the many variations of Judaism with which Roman administrators were familiar. As Jews enjoyed valuable privileges and exemptions within the empire it was important to know which Jewish movements really could be recognized by Rome. For this the Roman magistrates relied on the decisions of the Temple authorities in Jerusalem and on the protection afforded to Jewish groups by the puppet Jewish kings appointed by the Romans.

Jesus and his followers were thoroughly Jewish and never broke with mainstream Judaism even if the most rigid and fundamentalist Jews did accuse them of breaking some of the finer points of the law. In the Sermon on the Mount (Matt 5–7) Jesus urged people to return to the fundamental truths of Judaism, not abandon them. They observed the Jewish feasts faithfully, including the pilgrimages to Jerusalem and its Temple. Jesus interpreted his own mission by means of the teachings of the Old Testament prophets. 'I have not come to destroy the [Jewish] law and the prophets,' he said 'but to fulfill them'.

Arrested by order of the High Priest of Jerusalem just before Passover, AD 30, Jesus was condemned first on a blasphemy charge by the Jewish supreme court because he claimed to be the Son of God and Messiah, and then a treason charge. It was brought by the High Priest in the Roman court before Pontius Pilate because the Jewish court could not pass the death penalty. Reluctantly, Pilate had him crucified, the normal method of execution for condemned criminals. Jesus was declared dead and buried the same day. Three days later the empty tomb and appearances to his followers provided evidence for the most distinctive belief of Christians, the resurrection of Jesus from death.

Non-Jewish Christians

The number of people who accepted Jesus as the Jewish Messiah, risen from the dead, increased rapidly, but they had no intention of breaking with Judaism and continued to practise their Jewish faith in all its detail. In private they began to celebrate their beliefs about Jesus by repeating the ritual of the last Passover meal which Jesus presided over before his death, as 'the breaking of bread', but weekly instead of annually. They also adapted the rite some Jews practised of baptism—ritual washing in water—as a sign of forgiveness of sins and commitment to follow Jesus.

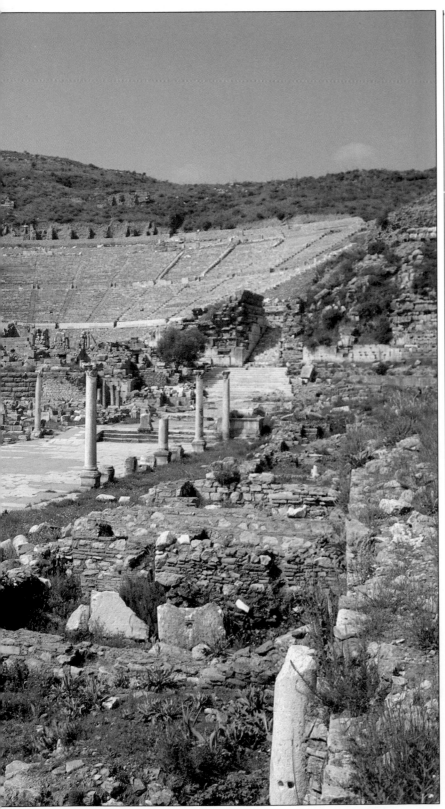

Doubts began to arise about Judaism as an appropriate way of life for all Christians as more and more non-Jews were received into the Christian communities. The conversion of Paul, a strict Jewish Pharisee, and his subsequent missionary work amongst the non-Jews of Asia Minor, brought matters to a head. Paul saw that converts should not be compelled to become Jews in order to be good Christians. If Christianity was to be the universal means of salvation it could not be restricted to any one culture, not even Judaism. It must be free from unnecessary restrictions.

Eighteen years after the death of Jesus the young Christian church accepted Paul's advice at a meeting of its leaders in Jerusalem. Christian converts did not have to conform to Jewish practices such as circumcision and the dietary laws, they only had to abstain from practices which were incompatible with fundamental Christian values.

Expansion into Europe

After the meeting of Christian leaders in Jerusalem to resolve the problems of non-Jews who became Christians, almost all the information in the New Testament concentrates on the journeys of Paul into Asia Minor and Europe until he reached Rome in AD 61.

Paul's first journey as a missionary for Christianity in AD 47 had taken him into Asia Minor, and on his second journey two years later he meant only to revisit the places where he had founded Christian churches. He changed his plans by going on to Troas, the busy port near the old site of Troy, where he and his companions—including Luke—sailed to Neapolis on the mainland of Europe. There they set out on the Via Egnatia, the main land route from Italy to the east, and began their dramatic mission through Macedonia and Greece.

LEFT *The Greek theatre in Ephesus, on the western slope of Mount Pion, could seat 24,000 people. Many Ephesians were later converted to Christianity which had to be presented to them and other non-Jews quite differently from the way it was presented to Jewish people.*

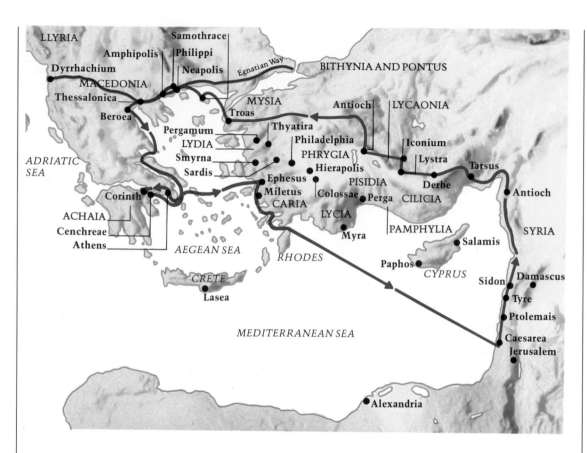

LLYRIA
Samothrace
Amphipolis
Philippi
Dyrrhachium
Neapolis
Egnatian Way
BITHYNIA AND PONTUS
MACEDONIA
Thessalonica
MYSIA
Antioch
LYCAONIA
Beroea
Troas
Pergamum
Thyatira
ADRIATIC
SEA
LYDIA
Philadelphia
Iconium
Smyrna
PHRYGIA
Lystra
Tarsus
Sardis
Hierapolis
Ephesus
PISIDIA
Derbe
Antioch
Corinth
Miletus
Colossae
Perga
CILICIA
ACHAIA
CARIA
LYCIA
SYRIA
Cenchreae
PAMPHYLIA
Athens
Myra
Salamis
AEGEAN SEA
RHODES
Damascus
Paphos
CYPRUS
Sidon
CRETE
Tyre
Lasea
Ptolemais
MEDITERRANEAN SEA
Caesarea
Jerusalem
Alexandria

LEFT *On his second journey Paul travelled west through Asia Minor as far as the Aegean area. This trip was probably the most important he made as it was then that he first preached the gospel in Europe. Paul founded many Christian communities on his way to Corinth.*

Paul's 2nd
— missionary
journey

BELOW RIGHT *Paul visited Athens in AD 50, and was invited to expound his teachings. His preaching proved too unsophisticated for Athenians, with his talk of a man being raised from the dead. Greek philosophy was later brought to the service of Christianity.*

Paul's 3rd
— missionary
journey

--- Paul's arrest and
journey to Rome

At Philippi, their first stop after Neapolis, Paul and Silas were arrested, flogged and imprisoned to await trial on a charge of advocating practices unlawful for Romans. But both men were 'Roman citizens', a status which should have protected them from such treatment, and they were released. At Thessalonica, Paul's party fled from the city when his new converts were accused of treason against Rome.

Athens

They were opposed again at the next town, so Paul went on to Athens. There Paul changed his tactics, and instead of starting in the local Jewish synagogue with teaching about Jesus as Messiah, he presented Christian beliefs in terms of Greek philosophy. For a while he held his audience at the foot of the Acropolis, but the resurrection of Jesus was too much for most of them, and Paul moved on to Corinth.

In Corinth, Paul and his companions found the response they had been looking for and they stayed there for 18 months. Leaving behind a thriving Christian church, Paul then returned to Palestine. After a short stay in his home church at Antioch he set off again for Asia Minor, where he passed through Galatia and Phrygia to stay for two years in Ephesus, the main adminstrative centre. His success was so great there that it threatened the trade in copies of the famous statue of Diana of the Ephesians, to whom the city was dedicated. When rioting broke out Paul decided to leave for Macedonia and Corinth again.

Paul in Rome

At Corinth, Paul decided that he should extend his work into the western parts of the Roman empire, and wrote a letter to the Christians of Rome to prepare his way. He journeyed back to Palestine to report his

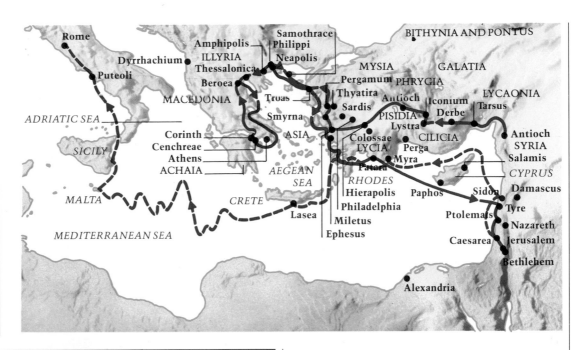

BITHYNIA AND PONTUS
Rome
Amphipolis — Samothrace
Philippi
Neapolis
ILLYRIA
Dyrrhachium
Thessalonica
MYSIA
GALATIA
Beroea
Puteoli
Pergamum
PHRYGIA
MACEDONIA
Troas
Thyatira
Antioch
Iconium
LYCAONIA
ADRIATIC SEA
Smyrna
Sardis
Derbe
Tarsus
PISIDIA
Corinth
ASIA
Lystra
Antioch
SICILY
Cenchreae
Colossae
CILICIA
SYRIA
Athens
LYCIA
Perga
Salamis
ACHAIA
AEGEAN
Patara
Myra
CYPRUS
SEA
RHODES
Paphos
Sidon
Damascus
MALTA
CRETE
Hierapolis
Tyre
Philadelphia
Ptolemais
Nazareth
MEDITERRANEAN SEA
Lasea
Miletus
Caesarea
Jerusalem
Ephesus
Bethlehem
Alexandria

RIGHT *Ephesus stood at the mouth of the River Cayster, which flows into the Aegean Sea. It was from here that Paul started his third missionary journey. He was based in Ephesus for two and a half years before writing the First Letter to the Corinthians and perhaps the Galatians. The Second Letter, which was followed by Paul's arrival (in the autumn of AD 50), arose after a crisis which developed among the Christians in Corinth. It was from Corinth that Paul wrote to the Romans, his most famous letter. As a result of charges brought against him by the Jewish religious authorities, Paul set out for Rome, to appeal as a Roman citizen to the Emperor Nero. Paul had originally intended to go to Rome and use it as a base for missionary work.*

progress to the Christian leaders in Jerusalem, still the main centre of the new faith.

The Palestine to which Paul returned in AD 58 was in ferment, eight years later this erupted into the disastrous war between the Jews and Rome in which Jerusalem was destroyed. Innocently enough, Paul went to the great Jewish Temple in Jerusalem to pray, as he had so often done in the past, and a crowd quickly gathered to lynch him because they thought he had taken non-Jews into parts of the Temple area from which they were excluded on pain of death.

The Roman guard stopped the riot by arresting Paul, and only his Roman citizenship saved him from interrogation under the lash. The senior Roman officer in Jerusalem decided to move Paul under a strong protective guard to the safety of the Roman administrative headquarters in Caesarea. Paul was held there for two years without trial. Finally, his patience exhausted, Paul exercised his rights as a Roman citizen and had his case transferred to Rome.

Shipwreck

Paul's voyage to Rome, guarded by a detachment of Roman soldiers, took the best part of a year. They first took a coastal vessel

MEDITERRANEAN SEA

PROVINCE
OF SYRIA

Caesarea Philippi

Capernaum
Gennesaret

Ptolemais (Acco)
SEA OF GALILEE
Mount Carmel ▲

Bethsaida-Julias
GALILEE
• Cana
Gergesa?
Hippos
TETRARCHY
OF PHILIP

THE GREAT PLAIN
• Nazareth
• Gadara
Tiberias

Dor
Caesarea
Roman headquarters

• Scythopolis
• Pella

JUDEA
• Gerasa
DECAPOLIS

• Sebaste
(Samaria)
R. Jabbok

Joppa
Alexandrium ★
Cyprus
R. Jordan

Ephraim
★ **Philadelphia**

Emmaus
Jericho ★
PEREA

Jerusalem
Bethlehem
Bethany ★
Medeba

Ashkelon
Herodium
Hebron •
Khirbet Qumran
'Dead Sea Scrolls'

Gaza
Hyrcania
★ **Machaerus**
R. Arnon

IDUMEA
Masada ★
NABATAEAN KINGDOM

Malatha

*LAKE ASPHALTITIS
(DEAD SEA)*

ABOVE *The Jewish–Roman war of AD 66–70 began with disturbances near Caesarea, the Roman administrative headquarters, and then spread throughout the country. The war was a severe test of the Roman occupation of Palestine; isolated pockets of resistance held out for more than three years. Many patriotic groups, such as the Zealots, were ready to commit suicide rather than surrender. These groups provided the main Jewish resistance to the Roman occupation. The Zealots' last stand was the royal stronghold of Masada which they held for nearly six years before it fell to the Romans in AD 73. The Romans overran Jerusalem in stages, and the Temple, held by the Zealots, was the last place to be captured. The burning of the Temple and destruction of Jerusalem marked the climax of the war.*

— Major trade routes
★ Fortresses

ABOVE *Jerusalem and the Hebrew University there are still the great centres of orthodox Jewish studies and worship. Paul himself studied the Jewish Law in Jerusalem before his dramatic conversion to Christianity.*

FAR LEFT *The famous statue of Diana at Ephesus (of which this is a copy made two centuries after Paul visited the city) who was worshipped in the fertility cult religions from which many Christian converts were made. The production of these sacred images of Diana was an important industry in the city.*

to Myra, and there transferred to one of the great grain ships which sailed between Egypt and Italy. Headwinds delayed them, then a storm drove them aground at Malta where the ship broke up. It was a further three months before the party reached Puteoli near Neapolis (Naples) on the Italian mainland. Paul found there were already Christians at Neapolis and stayed a week, then he and his guard travelled along the Appian Way to Nero's Rome. It was AD 61, three years before the great fire of Rome and Nero's persecution of the Roman Christians.

The Acts of the Apostles ends with Paul's arrival in Rome and the meetings he arranged with leading members of the Jewish community there. According to Acts he spent two years 'in his own rented lodging' waiting for his case to be heard in Nero's court, but it does not say whether he gained a hearing, nor what happened to him. Early Christian writings say that Paul was freed at the end of the two years in Rome, in which case he

could have carried out his plans to extend his missionary work westwards, at least as far as Spain. The same early traditions hold that Paul was eventually executed by Nero, at the same time as Peter.

War and Persecution

Fire broke out in Rome in the summer of AD 64, spread rapidly for six days and devastated 10 of the city's 14 wards. The Roman emperor, Nero, had begun his reign 10 years earlier with executions to secure his power. Until the fire there was no attempt to oppress Christians, even though the emperors were already worshipped as divine and the 16-year-old Nero encouraged the cult.

The Christians in Rome were convenient scapegoats for the fire, and Nero had many put to death with sadistic cruelty, not only for the fire but because they were 'haters of

the human race' who refused to take part in other religious rites. Many of the executions took place in the Vatican Gardens belonging to the emperor, near where St Peter's now stands. These persecutions were confined to Rome, but they created a precedent for Roman officials in other parts of the empire. Rejected by the Jewish authorities as well, Christians could no longer expect to be ignored in times of trouble.

Nero's reign ended in chaos and a year of civil war in Rome. Roman troops burned the Capitol, three emperors were proclaimed and overthrown, and eventually Vespasian emerged as victor to reign as emperor from AD 68 to 79. In Palestine the situation rapidly deteriorated in the war which had broken out between Rome and the Jews of the extreme nationalistic parties.

LEFT Rome was the greatest city in the world, dominating the whole of the Mediterranean area in Paul's day. The Forum and the Capitol in Rome were the centre of the empire, symbols of the authority vested in the Emperor, to whom Paul was appealing for justice.

BELOW Titus's victory in the Jewish–Roman War and his conquest of Jerusalem in AD 70 are commemorated by this triumphal arch erected by his brother Domitian at the old entrance to the Palatine in Rome.

Jerusalem Levelled

Vespasian had been put in charge of the Roman troops in Palestine and by the time he was proclaimed emperor he had subdued all of Judea and Idumea. The Jewish religious community at Qumran hid its library in nearby caves and fled to the massive fortress of Masada, which was held by the zealots. The Romans besieged Jerusalem.

Vespasian's son Titus took over when his father was proclaimed emperor, and captured Jerusalem in AD 70 after the destruction of the Temple by its fanatical defenders. The city was levelled and its surviving citizens sold into slavery. Further strongholds fell during the years AD 70–73, including the massive fortresses built by the Herods: the Herodium, Machaerus and Masada. The long defence of Masada has passed into Jewish legend.

The Romans rebuilt Jerusalem but they forbade Jews to live there and the Temple has never been rebuilt. The Christians of Jerusalem fled the city before the Romans besieged it, and settled at Pella in the Jordan valley near where the river leaves the Sea of Galilee. From now on, Jerusalem would no longer be the main centre of authority for the Christians of the Roman empire. The Christians who had left Jerusalem came under local attack from both Jews and Romans, but the only further serious persecution during New Testament times did not occur until the reign of the emperor Domitian near the end of the first century.

The Revelation to John

The Book of Revelation is different from any other in the New Testament both in its style and in its contents, because it is written in code. Like similar writings in the Old Testament, the writer of it was trying to encourage people under persecution, but had to do so in a way which would not increase their sufferings at the hands of the ruling powers.

The persecuted Christians to whom John wrote from his prison island off the coast of Asia Minor, would know that the people and places named in the book were a code for the

powers who were oppressing them. 'Babylon' symbolized Rome, 'the seven heads of the beast' were Rome's seven hills, and so on. If the work fell into the hands of the Roman authorities it could not be used against them as evidence of treason.

Although it is cryptic in its details, the general teaching of the Book of Revelation is clear enough. Whatever forces may appear to be ruling the world, their powers are illusory and transitory, so they can never really defeat God and his faithful people. The heavenly Jerusalem will become the capital of a new world, and all faithful Christians will be citizens of it. Even the might of Rome at the height of its powers and glory will be unable to prevent God from completing his plans for the salvation of the world under his personal rule.

RIGHT *The Book of Revelation was written about* AD 60 – *during the persecution of the Christians by the Emperor Domitian – on the prison island of Patmos, probably by John, the putative author of John's Gospel. The language used is a carefully disguised code giving counsel and warnings. Christians with a knowledge of the Old Testament would easily have recognized the description of Babylon as referring to the Roman state, but the Romans would have found it difficult to prove that the Book was critical of them.*

—— *Egnatian Way*

✝ *Asia's 'Seven churches'*

LEFT AND FAR LEFT *Qumran caves, on the north-west shore of the Dead Sea, in present day Jordan. At the height of the Jewish–Roman war, the Jewish scholars of Qumran hid their library in the caves and fled to the fortress of Masada. The discovery of the Qumran scrolls, written or copied in the first century* BC *and the first half of the first century* AD, *has given valuable insights into Judaism in the time of Jesus.*

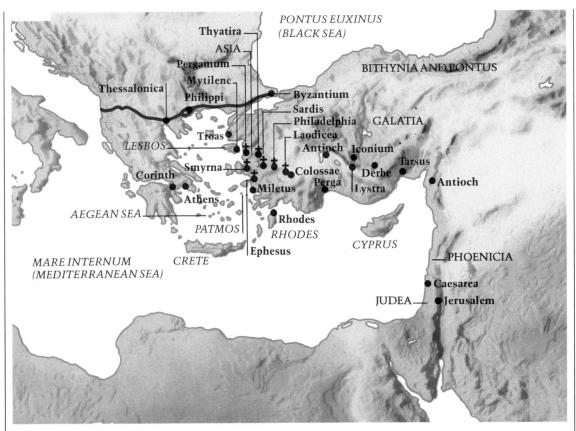

Recognition by Rome

From its bases in the Greek-speaking world, Christianity spread into Mesopotamia, Persia and India. Soon it was firmly established in western Europe, including Britain, and for most of the time Christians were allowed to practise their religion without interference, even though there are records of two widespread persecutions by the Roman authorities in AD 250 and 303. In AD 313 the joint Roman emperors Constantine and Licinius gave legal recognition to Christianity.

When Constantine moved the capital of the Roman empire from Rome to Constantinople in AD 331 he hoped that Christianity would unite all his subjects, for the empire was beginning to disintegrate. The differences between Greek-speaking Christians and Latin-speaking Christians had become more serious. In AD 325 a council held at Nicea tried to close the widening breach with a creed which set out the basic beliefs of Christianity. Six more 'ecumenical' councils during the following four and a half centuries would try to establish a form of Christanity faithful to its founder and agreed by all Christians.

Roman Symbols

As the need grew for a clear organizational structure, Christianity adopted symbols of authority and administrative practices from the Romans—a 'diocese' was originally a secular administrative region of the Roman empire. The special status of the Bishop of Rome was recognized at the Council of Constance in AD 451 after the Bishop of Constantinople had appealed to him for a summary of the Christian faith.

Monasticism developed when hermits in the Egyptian desert adopted a common rule of life. It soon spread as far as Britain, where Patrick used it as the means of consolidating Christianity in Ireland. Ninian and Columba then took monasticism from Ireland to

mosques, such as the Dome of the Rock in Jerusalem built on the site of the Jewish Temple destroyed in AD 70. Islam accepts both the Old Testament and the New Testament as the revealed will of God, but holds that they have both been superseded by the revelations dictated by God to Mohammed through the angel Gabriel, which became the Islamic sacred scriptures, the Koran.

The Bible Lands Today

The Near and Middle East is still predominantly Islamic in faith with pockets of Christianity, with the exception of Israel, and even Israel has a large Islamic population. Jerusalem contains the sacred sites of three great religions, Judaism, Christanity and Islam. It is hardly surprising that it still attracts millions of religious pilgrims each year as visible proof of the importance of the Bible and the Koran to people all over the modern world.

Palestine, Lebanon and western Syria remain vitally important strategic areas along the eastern coast of the Mediterranean, no longer as links between Egypt and Mesopotamia, but because areas nearby produce most of the world's oil. The pipelines across the Arabian Desert have taken the place of the old caravan routes whenever the recurrent wars leave them intact.

From Egypt to Mesopotamia, the careful distribution of water to the agricultural lands by irrigation remains as important as ever. This can be seen from the Aswan High Dam in Egypt, which helps control the annual floods of the River Nile on which Egypt still depends. In Palestine, modern methods of agriculture and new techniques of irrigation are producing crops in parts of the country previously thought useless for cultivation.

The Arabian Desert is still an area where nomadic herding continues as a way of life little changed over the centuries. The brief period of lush growth after rain, followed by months of sparse scrub, supports herds of sheep and camels whose milk and meat provide for the desert nomads. Abraham would be baffled by the presence everywhere of modern technology, but he would recognize the essential pattern of the nomad's way of life as little different from his own.

Scotland. The Benedictine form of monasticism spread rapidly and was introduced into England by Augustine of Canterbury in AD 597.

Islam

The greatest setback to the continued spread of Christianity came from the Arabian desert, where Mohammed was born in Mecca about AD 570. He preached Islam (which means 'surrender' — to God), a strict monotheism which taught that Allah is the sole God of the universe who alone must be worshipped. Mohammed had to use force to overcome the antagonism of the families which controlled western Arabia, but Islam was (and still is) outstandingly successful because it provided its adherents with such a simple and coherent way of worship and life.

With remarkable speed Islam swept through northern Africa, Palestine, Asia Minor and parts of Europe, and marked its progress with breathtakingly beautiful shrines and

ABOVE *Date palms have been growing near the Tigris and Euphrates rivers for over 4,000 years. Throughout this period, up until the present day, the date palm has been a major source of food.*

LEFT *The Biblical lands have never been at peace, the conflict still continues. Palestine is the key to the Near and Middle East, not only because of the vast quantities of oil, but because battlefields such as Lebanon still exist. The weapons have changed, but the struggle continues.*

RIGHT *The Dome of the Rock by night. It was the first domical mosque and is laid out on the basic Byzantine octagonal plan. Built in the 7th century, the Dome of the Rock protects an outcrop of rock where King Solomon's Temple stood. It is a striking reminder of the progress of Islam so soon after the death of Mohammed.*

Appendices

3000	2500	

3000-2600 BC Semitic shepherds in Mesopotamia and Arabian desert

MESOPOTAMIA

2600-2130 BC Sume

2130-

EGYPT

3000-2600 BC 1st-3rd Dynasties

2600-2130 BC Old K

2130

Hyksos rulers expelled; Egypt united; wars with Mi

3100-2100 BC
Canaanites

PALESTINE

213

outh-east; Akkadians begin to dominate from Babylon

0 BC Sumerian revival; Amorites in west; Assyria briefly dominant

c1724-1595 BC Old Babylonian Empire; Hurrians in north; Persians in east

c1724-1686 BC Reign of Hammurabi

c1720 BC Code of Hammurabi

c1595-1360 BC Mitanni in north, Hurrians under Aryan rulers; Assyria controls central Mesopotamia; Kassites overthrow Babylon

Assyria dominant under Tiglath-pileser I c1100 BC

21st Dynasty, capital: Tanis 1070-945 BC

h-8th Dynasties, capital: Memphis; first completed pyramids

t Intermediate Period, 9th-11th Dynasties, capitals: Heracleopolis and Thebes

2030-1640 BC Middle Kingdom, 11th-14th Dynasties, capitals: Memphis and Thebes

1640-1530 BC 2nd Intermediate Period; 15th-16th Dynasties, Hyksos kings, capital: Avaris (Tanis); 17th Dynasty, capital: Thebes; Hittites in Asia Minor

New Kingdom, 18th-20th Dynasties, capital: Thebes; 1550-1070 BC

c1358-1349 BC Reign of Tut'ankhamun

Akhnaton tries to impose monotheism; capital: Tell el-Amarna 1360 BC

Reign of Rameses II, capital: Pi-Rameses 1290-1224 BC

20th Dynasty 1194-1070 BC

Reign of Rameses III 1194-1163 BC

Victory over the 'Sea Peoples' 1175 BC

BC Canaanites; Amorites in north; Egypt controls coastal region

c1800-1600 BC Abraham, Isaac and Jacob

1640-1530 BC Hebrew groups settle in Egypt on borders of Canaan

Canaanites under Egyptian control 1550-1070 BC

Hebrew groups settle in northern, central and southern Canaan c1360 BC

Battle of Kadesh, narrow Egyptian victory over Hittites 1285 BC

Hebrew escape from Egypt (the exodus) 1250 BC

Hebrew domination of Canaan begins under Joshua 1220-1200 BC

Philistines occupy the Palestinian coast 1200-900 BC

The Judges c1200-1025 BC

Reign of David c1010-970 BC

Reign of Saul c1030-1010 BC

Samuel c1040 BC

Victory of the Philistines at Aphek c1050 BC

RIA

ME AND GREECE   Aramaean kingdoms of Damascus, Zobah, Hamath etc c1100 BC

A MINOR AND BEYOND   Trojan War 1194-1184 BC

	1000	900	800
MESOPOTAMIA			

EGYPT

945-924 BC Reign of Sheshonk I, his campaign in Palestine

945-725 BC 22nd Dynasty, capital: Bubastis

PALESTINE

● c1000 BC Capture of Jerusalem

841-835 BC (Judah) Reign of Athaliah

835-796 BC (Judah) Reign o

c970-931 BC Reign of Solomon

814-798 BC (Israel) Reign of Je

931-910 BC (Israel) Reign of Jeroboam I

798-783 BC (Israel) R

931-913 BC (Judah) Reign of Rehoboam

796-781 BC (Judah)

913-911 BC (Judah) Reign of Abijah

841-814 BC (Israel) Reign of Jehu

911-870 BC (Judah) Reign of Asa

910-909 BC (Israel) Reign of Nadab

909-886 BC (Israel) Reign of Baasha

886-885 BC (Israel) Reign of Elah

● 885 BC (Israel) Zimri rules for seven days

885-874 BC (Israel) Reign of Omri; founding of Samaria

874-853 BC (Israel) Reign of Ahab; Elijah

870-848 BC (Judah) Reign of Jehoshaphat

853-852 BC (Israel) Reign of Ochozias

852-841 BC (Israel) Reign of Jehoram; Elisha

848-841 BC (Judah) Reign of Jehoram

Capt

SYRIA

Hazael, king of Damascus, defeated by Shalmaneser III 841 BC ●

Tiglath-pileser III receives tribute from Rezin, king of Damas

ROME AND GREECE

● c7

ASIA MINOR AND BEYOND

● 841 BC (Assyria) Shalmaneser III reaches the sea

883-859 BC Revival of Assyria, reign of Ashurnasirpal

858-824 BC (Assyria) Reign of Shalmaneser III

● 853 BC Battle at Qarqar

704-681 BC Reign of Sennacherib

● 701 BC Sennacherib defeats Egyptians at Eltekeh and captures Lachish

680-669 BC Reign of Esarhaddon

626-539 BC Neo-Babylonian Dynasty

626-605 BC Reign of Nebupolassar

● 609 BC Nebupolassar repulses the army of Necho II

● 605 BC Crown prince Nebuchadnezzar defeats Necho's armies at Carchemish

c750 BC Rivalry between 22nd Dynasty (capital: Bubastis) and 23rd Dynasty (capital: Thebes)

669-630 BC Reign of Ashurbanipal

556-539 BC Reign of Nabonidus

Cyrus II captures Babylon 539 BC ●

724-715 BC 24th Dynasty, capital: Sais

605-562 BC Reign of Nebuchadnezzar

715-663 BC 25th Dynasty, capital: Nubia

685-664 BC Reign of Tirhakah

● c671 BC Esarhaddon takes control of Lower Egypt

750 BC (Israel) Amos and Hosea

● 668 BC Ashurbanipal pushes Tirhakah back beyond Thebes

● 743 BC (Israel) Reign of Shallum

● 663 BC The sacking of Thebes

ash ● 740 BC (Judah) Isaiah

663-525 BC 26th Dynasty, capital: Sais

maziah

663-609 BC Reign of Psammetichus I

781-740 BC (Israel) Reign of Uzziah

● c650 BC Psammetichus I drives the Assyrians out of Egypt

● 743 BC (Israel) Reign of Zechariah

609-594 BC Reign of Necho II

743-738 BC (Israel) Reign of Menahem

● 601 BC Nebuchadnezzar is defeated in Egypt

740-736 BC (Judah) Reign of Jotham; Micah

● c 630 BC Zephaniah

594-589 BC Reign of Psammetichus II

738-737 BC (Israel) Reign of Pekahiah

642-640 BC Reign of Amon

589-570 BC Reign of Apries (Hophra)

737-732 BC (Israel) Reign of Pekah

Beginning of reign of Psammetichus III 525 BC ●

735-715 BC (Judah) Reign of Ahaz; Rezin and Pekah besiege Jerusalem; Isaiah's prophecy of Emmanuel

● c734 BC Tiglath-pileser III captures part of Galilee

640-609 BC Reign of Josiah

732-724 BC (Israel) Reign of Hoshea

● 627 BC Call of Jeremiah

582-581 BC Further exile to Babylon

724-722 BC Samaria besieged by Shalmaneser V

● 622 BC Religious reform

715-687 BC Reign of Hezekiah

● c612 BC Nahum

● 711 BC Sargon captures Ashdod

● 609 BC Reign of Jehoahaz

c704 BC Hezekiah pays tribute to Sennacherib

609-598 BC Reign of Jehoiakim

687-642 BC Reign of Manasseh ● 588 BC Diversion by Apries

604-587 BC Nebuchadnezzar conquers Palestine

● 600 BC Revolt of Jehoiakim; Habukkuk

598-597 BC Reign of Jehoiachin

597-587 BC Reign of Zedekiah

● 589 BC Revolt of Zedekiah, siege of Jerusalem

struction of Jerusalem, exile to Babylon; assassination of the governor of Judah, Gedaliah 587 BC ●

● c732 BC Tiglath-pileser III leads campaign against Rezin

Foundation of the Second Temple 537 BC ●

738 BC ● ● c732 BC End of independence of Damascus

The Edict of Cyrus, return from Babylon 538 BC ●

Building of the Second Temple; Zerubbabel is high commissioner; Joshua is high priest; Haggai and Zechariah 520-515 BC

nding of Rome

(Greece) Life of Pythagoras 570-497 BC

Roman Republic declared 509 BC ●

721-705 BC (Assyria) Reign of Sargon II; 721 BC he captures Samaria, inhabitants deported; he defeats Sibe, of Egypt

Nebupolassar and Cyaxares, king of Medes, take and destroy Nineveh 612 BC ● ● 606 BC Nebupolassar ends the Assyrian Empire

(Persia) Reign of Cyrus II 555-529 BC

783-745 BC Assyria weak

Cyrus II captures Ecbatana 550 BC ●

754-727 BC (Assyria) Reign of Tiglath-pileser III

Cyrus II captures Sardis and Pteria 546 BC ●

726-722 BC (Assyria) Reign of Shalmaneser V

(Persia) Reign of Cambyses' 529-522 BC

	500	480	460	440	420	400	380	360

EGYPT

● *c*400 BC Egyptians reinstate self rule

PALESTINE

498-399 BC Obadiah

486-423 BC Malachi and Obadiah

445-443 BC First mission of Nehemiah; before 423 BC second mission of Nehemiah

● 398 BC Ezra's mission

SYRIA

ROME AND GREECE

499-479 BC War between Greece and Persia

● 490 BC Battle of Marathon

*c*469-399 BC (Greece) Life of Socrates

461-429 BC (Greece) Life of Pericles

*c*427-347 BC (Greece) Life of Plato

384-322 BC (Greece) Life of Aristotl

ASIA MINOR AND BEYOND

522-486 BC (Persia) Reign of Darius

486-465 BC (Persia) Reign of Xerxes I

465-423 BC (Persia) Reign of Artaxerxes I Longimanus

(Persia) Reign of Xerxes II 423 BC ●

404-358 BC

423-404 BC (Persia) Reign of Darius II Nothus

400-343 BC 28th-30th Dynasties

Reign of Ptolemy V Epiphanes 204-180 BC

● 331 BC Foundation of Alexandria

304-30 BC Egypt is ruled by Ptolemies

304-284 BC Reign of Ptolemy I Soter

285-246 BC Reign of Ptolemy II Philadelphus

276-273 BC Egypt at war with Syria

Reign of Ptolemy III Euergetes 246-221 BC

Reign of Ptolemy IV Philopator 221-205 BC

Before 336 BC Joel; Chronicles; Ezra-Nehemiah

c336-331 BC Jonah; Tobit

● 332 BC Alexander captures Tyre and Gaza; he enters Egypt

304-200 BC Judea is ruled by Ptolemies

● c246 BC Esther and Ecclesiastes

Egyptian victory over Antiochus III at Raphia 217 BC ●

Antiochus III reconquers Palestine 202-200 BC

c305-125 BC Seleucid Dynasty

c305-281 BC Reign of Seleucus I Nicator

281-261 BC Reign of Antiochus I Soter

● 333 BC Alexander conquers Syria

261-246 BC Reign of Antiochus II Theos

Reign of Seleucus II Callinicos 246-226 BC

Reign of Seleucus III Ceraunus 226-223 BC

Reign of Antiochus III the Great 223-187 BC

336-323 BC (Greece) Reign of Alexander the Great

333-63 BC The Hellenist Period

● 323 BC Alexander dies in Babylon

● c305 BC (Greece) Foundation of the Epicurean and Stoic schools

First Punic War between Rome and Carthage 264-241 BC

● 241 BC Romans conquer Sicily

Romans conquer Sardinia and Corsica 238 BC ●

Hannibal's land campaigns against Rome 219-202 BC

Second Punic War between Rome and Carthage 218-201 BC

Hannibal's land campaigns against Rome 209-207 BC

sia) Reign of Artaxerxes II Mnemon ● 301 BC Battle of Ipsus

● 331 BC Alexander ends the Persian Empire

330-326 BC Alexander conquers the eastern satrapies and India

200	180	160	140	120

MESOPOTAMIA

171-138 BC Reign of Mithridates I Arsaces I, king of the Pa▮

141 BC Mithridates takes Seleucia (on the Tigris) and Babylo▮

EGYPT

PALESTINE

200-142 BC Judea ruled by the Seleucids; Antiochus III confirm▮

c189-175 BC Simon II (the Just) is high priest; then Onias III is high priest

174-171 BC Jason is high priest

171 BC Menelaus is high priest, he has Onias III killed

167-164 BC The great persecution; sacrifices made to Olympian Zeus in the Temple; revolt of

166-160 BC Judas Maccabeus continues the revolt

c164 BC Book of Daniel

164 BC Purification of the Temple

c162 BC Judas Maccabeus allied with Rome

160 BC Nicanor defeated

160-143 BC Jonathan leads the Jews

152 BC Jonathan is made high priest

145 BC Charter of Demetrius II confirms Jonathan as ruler of Judea

143-134 BC Simon ruler of Judea

c141 BC Renewal of alliances with Rome and Sparta

104

103

SYRIA

190 BC Antiochus III defeated at Magnesia

c130 BC Formation of the Essene communit▮

187-175 BC Reign of Seleucus IV Philopator

175-164 BC Reign of Antiochus IV Epiphanes

164-161 BC Reign of Antiochus V Eupator

161-150 BC Reign of Demetrius I Soter

145-140 BC First reign of Demetrius II

144-142 BC Antiochus IV installed in Antioch

142-138 BC Tryphon succeeds Antiochus VI in Antioch

129-125 BC Second reign of Demetrius▮

197 BC Flaminius of Rome defeats Philip V of Macedonia; Spain conquered by Rome

ROME AND GREECE

149-146 BC Third Punic War between Rome and Carthage

148 BC Macedonia becomes a Roman province

146 BC Romans destroy Carthage and Corinth

133 BC Attalus III, king of Pergamum, bequeaths h▮

ASIA MINOR AND BEYOND

c150 BC Mithridates is ruler of almost all Persia

40 BC Parthians in Syria and Palestine

38 BC Parthians driven from Syria and Palestine

51-30 BC Reign of Cleopatra VII

30 BC Suicide of Antony and Cleopatra, Egypt becomes a Roman province

heocratic status of the Jews

tathias

n of Aristobulus I

n of Alexander Jannaeus

c Judith

76-67 BC Reign of Alexandra

67-63 BC Reign of Aristobulus II, he is also high priest

63 BC Pompey takes Jerusalem; Idumaean Antipator is real ruler of Judea

54 BC Crassus pillages the Temple

c 50 BC Wisdom

47 BC Herod is named strategos of Galilee

41 BC Herod and Phasael are made tetrarchs

nran

37 BC Capture of Jerusalem by Herod and Sosius

37-4 BC Reign of Herod the Great

Rebuilding of the Temple begins 20 BC

Birth of Jesus c 7 BC

Death of Herod 4 BC

95-88 BC Reign of Demetrius III (at Damascus)

63 BC Pompey at Damascus

te to Rome

67 BC Crete and Cyrenaica become a Roman province

66-62 BC Pompey in the east; Pontus and Bithynia become Roman provinces

64 BC Pompey deposes Philip II and Syria becomes a Roman province

55 BC Romans invade Britain

48 BC (Rome) Julius Caesar defeats Pompey

44 BC (Rome) Caesar assassinated

40 BC Roman senate names Herod 'King of Judea'

(Rome) Octavian defeats Antony at Actium 31 BC

Octavian is made Imperator of Rome for life 29 BC

Octavian is made emperor and named Augustus Caesar 27 BC

Galatia becomes a Roman province 25 BC

70 BC Tigranes, king of Armenia, dominates Syria

0	20	40	60	80	100	120	140	160	180	20

EGYPT AD 38 Persecution of Jews in Alexandria

4 BC-AD 39 Herod Antipas is tetrarch of Galilee and Perea; Philip is tetrarch of Gaulanitis, Batanaca, Trachonitis and Aurani

AD 6-14 Judea is a prefectorial province of Rome

PALESTINE cAD 26-36 Pontius Pilate is procurator

AD 27 John the Baptist preaching and the beginning of the ministry of Jesus

AD 30 Death of Jesus; outpouring of the Spirit of the Church

cAD 34-36 Martyrdom of Stephen; conversion of Paul

AD 53-58 Third mission of Paul

AD 58-60 Paul held at Caesarea

AD 67-68 The Zealots are masters of Jerusalem

cAD 39 Peter in Samaria   cAD 75 Gospel of Matthew; Gospel of Luke; Acts of Apostles; the Letter of Jude

AD 41-48 Herod becomes king of Chalcis

AD 44-46 Judea again a prefectorial province of Rome

AD 70 Judea an imperial province of Rome

AD 45-49 First mission of Paul   cAD 95 2 Peter; Gospel of John; 1 John (3 John and 2 John possibly earlier); Revel

cAD 48 Famine in Judea; the Council of Jerusalem

AD 49-52 Second mission of Paul   116 Rebellion against Romans leads to dispersion of Jews

AD 50-52 Letters to the Thessalonians

AD 66 Jerusalem attacked by Cestius Gallius; Christians take refuge in Pella

AD 66-70 Jewish war against Romans

AD 67 Vespasian reconquers Galilee

cAD 67 Paul a prisoner in Rome; 2 Timothy; Paul is beheaded; Letter to the Hebrews

cAD 57 First Letter to the Corinthians; AD 57 second Letter to the Corinthians; Letter to the Galatians; Letter

AD 58 James's Letter to the Jews of the Dispersion; Paul arrested in the Temple

AD 69 Vespasian subdues Judea but the Zealots hold out in Jerusalem, Herodium, Masada and Macha

AD 60 Paul appears before Festus and appeals to Caesar; he starts his voyage to Rome

AD 61-63 Paul in Rome; Letters to Colossians, Ephesians, Philemon, and Philippians(?)

AD 70 Titus lays siege to Jerusalem, burning of the Temple, capture of the Upper City and the Palace

cAD 63 Paul set free(?); Gospel of Mark and 1 Peter; Letter of James; 1 Timothy; Letter to Titus?

AD 66 Florus crucifies some Jews in Jerusalem; troubles in Caesarea and throughout country

AD 14-37 (Rome) Emperor Tiberius

AD 37-41 (Rome) Emperor Caligula

ROME AND GREECE AD 41-54 (Rome) Emperor Claudius

AD 54-68 (Rome) Emperor Nero

AD 64 Burning of Rome, persecution of Christians

AD 64-67 Martyrdom of Peter at Rome

AD 66-67 Nero in Greece; he appoints Vespasian and Titus to restore order in Palestine

AD 68 (Rome) Galba is emperor; Nero commits suicide

AD 69 (Rome) Otho proclaimed emperor by the Praetorians, Vitellius proclaimed emperor by the legi

AD 69-79 (Rome) Emperor Vespasian

AD 79-81 (Rome) Emperor Titus

AD 96-98 (Rome) Emperor Nerva

AD 98-117 (Rome) Emperor Trajan

AD 81-96 (Rome) Emperor Domitian

117 The Roman Empire reaches its greatest extent

117 Christians martyred in Lyon (Gaul)

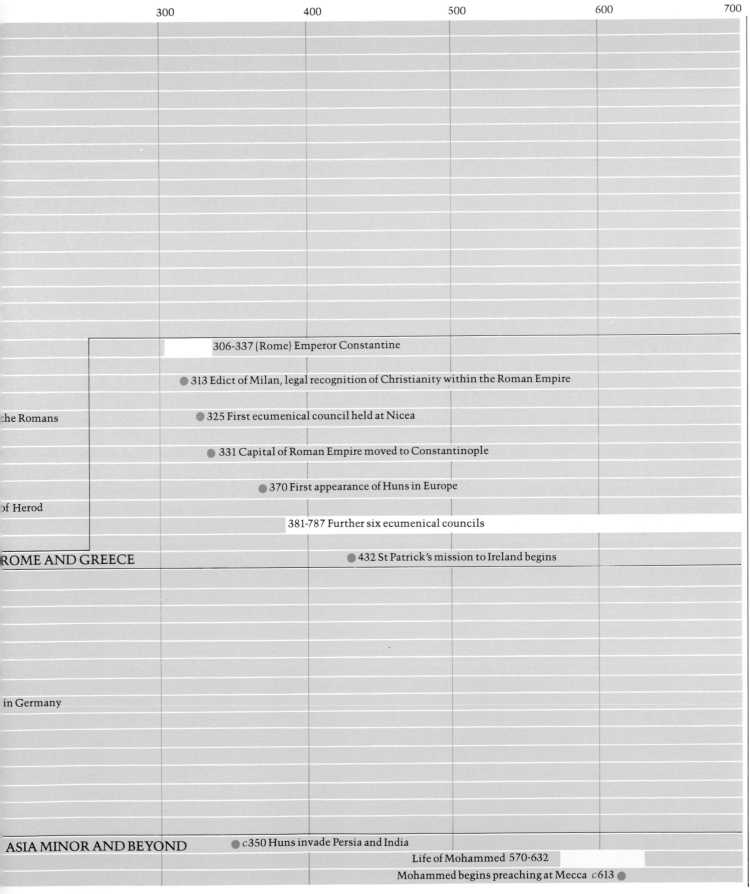

	300	**400**	**500**	**600**	**700**

306-337 (Rome) Emperor Constantine

● 313 Edict of Milan, legal recognition of Christianity within the Roman Empire

the Romans

● 325 First ecumenical council held at Nicea

● 331 Capital of Roman Empire moved to Constantinople

● 370 First appearance of Huns in Europe

of Herod

381-787 Further six ecumenical councils

ROME AND GREECE

● 432 St Patrick's mission to Ireland begins

in Germany

ASIA MINOR AND BEYOND   ● c350 Huns invade Persia and India

Life of Mohammed 570-632

Mohammed begins preaching at Mecca c613 ●

Italic page numbers refer to the illustrations.
Bold numbers refer to the maps.